Retirement Planning Guidebook

Proven Strategies and a Step-by-Step Blueprint for a Confident and Stress-Resilient Retirement

Jasper kensington

Table Of Contents

Introduction

Imagine this: You've spent decades building a career, raising a family, and navigating life's ups and downs. Now, after years of hard work, the finish line is in sight—retirement. But instead of feeling excited about finally relaxing and enjoying the fruits of your labor, there's a lingering question: *Am I really ready?*

If you're like most seniors and professionals approaching retirement, you've probably felt a mix of anticipation and anxiety. You've saved, invested, and tried to plan for the future, but the shifting economic landscape, increasing healthcare costs, and longer life expectancy have made retirement planning more complex than ever before. The truth is, the dream of a secure, stress-free retirement can often feel just out of reach.

This book was written to change that.

The Problem Many Face:

Consider David, a 62-year-old professional who thought he had everything figured out. He diligently saved in his 401(k), paid off his home, and was looking forward to a comfortable retirement. But as his retirement date approached, David began to worry about things he hadn't considered: How much would healthcare really cost? Were his investments strong enough to withstand another market downturn? Would his savings last through his retirement years?

David's concerns are not unique. Many soon-to-be retirees find themselves facing similar uncertainties. They wonder if their money will outlast them, if they've accounted for all potential expenses, and if their financial strategy is truly solid enough to support the lifestyle they want.

The *Retirement Planning Guidebook* is here to provide clarity in the face of these overwhelming questions.

Your Blueprint for a Secure Retirement:

This book isn't just another collection of financial tips. It's a comprehensive guide designed to help you build a personalized blueprint for your retirement, one that takes into account your unique needs, goals, and concerns. Whether you're worried about healthcare costs, managing investments, estate planning, or simply ensuring you don't outlive your savings, this guide breaks down complex topics into clear, actionable steps.

By following the strategies outlined in this book, you can move from a place of uncertainty to one of confidence and peace of mind. Imagine the relief of knowing that you've created a plan that's designed to weather market fluctuations, cover healthcare expenses, and allow you to enjoy your retirement years without constantly worrying about money.

Take the First Step Toward a Confident Retirement:

The journey to a secure and fulfilling retirement starts now. The pages ahead are filled with proven strategies and expert advice designed to help you take control of your financial future. I encourage you to read on, take notes, and start applying these principles today.

Together, we'll transform uncertainty into clarity, and anxiety into confidence. Let's start building your retirement blueprint—one that will empower you to live the life you've worked so hard for.

Welcome to your guide to a secure, confident retirement!

Understanding Retirement Planning: More Than Just Saving

Retirement planning is a thorough process that extends beyond simply conserving money. It entails a planned strategy for ensuring financial security and a satisfying lifestyle during your retirement years. The following's a closer look at what retirement planning entails.

1. Establishing clear goals

The first phase in retirement planning is setting your goals for retirement. Determine the age at which you intend to retire, the lifestyle you want to maintain, and any specific goals you have, such as travel or hobbies. Clear goals give a road map for your financial planning endeavors.

2. Estimating Future Expenditures

Understanding your future expenses is critical. This includes daily living expenses, healthcare charges, taxes, and any other expenditures. Estimating these costs allows you to better understand how much you need to save and invest to maintain your desired lifestyle.

3. Diversifying income sources.

Depending only on savings is inadequate. Diversifying your income streams is critical for a secure retirement. This can include pensions, social security benefits, rental income, part-time work, and investment returns. A diverse income stream decreases the possibility of a financial deficit.

4. Investment Strategies.

Investing intelligently is an essential part of retirement planning. This entails choosing the correct combination of assets, such as stocks, bonds, and real estate, to help you build wealth over time. The investment approach should be consistent with your risk tolerance and time horizon. Regularly monitoring and changing your portfolio is also essential for staying on track with your goals.

5. Tax Planning.

Effective tax preparation can have a big impact on retirement funds. Understanding the tax consequences of your retirement accounts, such as 401(k), IRAs, and Roth IRAs, can help you maximize your distributions while minimizing your tax liabilities. Strategic tax planning helps you keep more of your hard-earned money.

6. Healthcare considerations

Healthcare is a significant expense in retirement. Planning for healthcare costs, such as insurance premiums, out-of-pocket payments, and long-term care, is critical. Exploring choices such as Medicare and supplemental insurance can help you handle these costs more efficiently.

7. Estate Planning.

Estate planning guarantees that your possessions are dispersed how you intend after your death. This includes drafting a will, establishing trusts, and naming beneficiaries. Proper estate planning can also help to reduce estate taxes and legal difficulties for your heirs.

8. Regular Reviews and Adjustments.

Retirement preparation is not a one-time activity. It necessitates regular evaluations and adjustments to reflect changes in your financial state, market conditions, and personal objectives. Staying proactive and adaptive ensures that your retirement plan is still current and effective.

Retirement planning is a comprehensive process that includes establishing clear goals, calculating future needs, diversifying income sources, investing prudently, planning for taxes and healthcare, and ensuring appropriate estate planning. Taking a balanced strategy helps ensure a financially comfortable and pleasant retirement.

The Importance of a Comprehensive Approach

A comprehensive approach is important in many disciplines, including healthcare and education, because it guarantees that all parts of a problem or situation are treated holistically. This strategy is critical to generating long-term and successful results. **Here's why a holistic strategy is crucial:**

1. Holistic Understanding
A comprehensive approach enables thorough knowledge of the problem at hand. By taking into account all essential elements, it ensures that no important component is ignored. In healthcare, treating a patient's physical, mental and social requirements leads to improved overall health outcomes. Similarly, in education, emphasizing cognitive, emotional,

and social development helps pupils prepare for real-world challenges.

2. Improved Decision Making
When all factors in a scenario are evaluated, decision-making becomes more informed and effective. This decreases the likelihood of unforeseen repercussions and ensures that remedies are comprehensive. For example, in business, a thorough market study that encompasses economic, social, and technological variables can lead to more strategic and profitable judgments.

3. Enhanced Collaboration
A thorough approach frequently requires collaboration across disciplines and sectors. This encourages teamwork and the exchange of different ideas, resulting in more imaginative and effective solutions. In healthcare, for example, a multidisciplinary team approach can give more comprehensive care to patients by addressing multiple health problems at once.

4. Long-term sustainability.
Solutions created from a holistic approach are more likely to last in the long run. By addressing the core causes of problems rather

than just the symptoms, this strategy ensures that solutions are long-lasting and adaptable to future difficulties. In environmental management, for example, a comprehensive approach to conservation takes into account ecological, economic, and social aspects, leading to more sustainable practices.

5. Increased efficiency
While a thorough approach may require more initial time and resources, it frequently results in greater efficiency in the long term. Preventing problems from forming or increasing decreases the need for costly actions in the future. For example, thorough preventive healthcare can reduce the prevalence of chronic diseases, resulting in lower healthcare expenses over time.

6. Better outcomes.
Ultimately, a thorough strategy produces superior results. Whether in healthcare, education, business, or another profession, addressing all important elements ensures that solutions are both effective and helpful. This strategy not only improves individual outcomes, but it also benefits communities and societies as a whole.

The value of a comprehensive approach stems from its ability to provide holistic knowledge, improve decision-making, boost collaboration, assure long-term sustainability, increase efficiency, and achieve superior results. This approach, which takes into account all facets of a situation, results in more effective and durable solutions.

How to Use This Guidebook

Navigating the **"Retirement Planning Guidebook"** is simple, allowing readers to obtain the information they need based on their current level of retirement planning.

Below is a plan to help you get the most out of this guide:

Starting Out: Setting Goals and Assessing Your Situation.

If you're just getting started with retirement planning, Chapter 1: Defining Your Retirement Goals is a great place to start. This chapter will assist you in defining your ideal retirement lifestyle and setting clear, achievable goals. It also walks you through the process of reviewing your existing financial condition, which is critical for understanding where you are and what you need to accomplish your goals.

Building Your Retirement Income

Once you have a clear understanding of your objectives, proceed to Chapter 2: Building Your Retirement Income. This chapter discusses the fundamentals of a retirement income strategy, such as researching Social Security benefits, increasing employer contributions to pension programs, and developing a personal retirement portfolio. This is critical for anyone wanting to establish a consistent income stream during their retirement.

Managing Risks

For individuals concerned about the uncertainties of retirement, Chapter 3: Risk Management in Retirement is incredibly useful. It addresses how to assess market risks, manage longevity risk to ensure your income is sustainable, and plan for inflation. Understanding these dangers and how to mitigate them can bring you peace of mind and financial security.

Choosing Your Retirement Income Style.

If you're attempting to select how to manage your retirement assets, Chapter 4: Retirement Income Styles discusses income-focused versus growth-focused techniques. It helps you understand your financial mindset and balance risks by utilizing the Retirement Income Style Matrix to determine the best fit for you.

Evaluate Your Readiness

Chapter 5: The Funded Ratio Methodology is essential for determining your retirement readiness. It defines the funded ratio, explains why it is important, and provides a step-by-step formula for calculating it. This chapter will assist you in determining your retirement readiness and making any required adjustments.

Managing accounts and withdrawals

For those nearing or already retired, Chapter 6: Managing Retirement Accounts and Withdrawals provides ideas for tax-efficient withdrawals, understanding Traditional IRAs versus Roth IRAs, and avoiding RMD penalties.

Chapter 7: Healthcare and Long-Term Care Planning provides comprehensive discussion of healthcare costs, including Medicare and supplemental coverage, as well as long-term care insurance. This chapter guarantees that you are ready for medical bills in retirement.

Professional Advice versus Self-Management

If you're considering whether to manage your retirement money yourself or employ a professional, Chapter 8: Self-Managing Your Retirement vs. Hiring a Professional explains the benefits and drawbacks of each option, as well as how to select a financial advisor.

Estate Planning and Avoiding Pitfalls

Finally, Chapters 9: Estate Planning and Legacy Building and 10: Frequent Retirement Pitfalls and How to Avoid Them are critical for preserving your legacy and avoiding frequent blunders.

By following this guidance, you may personalize your retirement planning to your unique needs and life stage, resulting in a well-rounded and secure retirement.

Chapter 1:

Defining Your Retirement Goals

"The question isn't at what age I want to retire, it's at what income." – George Foreman

Defining specific retirement goals is an important step toward a comfortable and fulfilling retirement. This method takes into account a variety of factors, including your anticipated retirement age, lifestyle expectations, and personal financial goals. Here's a complete guide to helping you set these goals and assess your present financial situation.

Desired Retirement Age

The age at which you intend to retire has a considerable impact on retirement planning. Early retirement necessitates a larger savings pool due to the extended term of unemployment. Conversely, retiring later gives you more time to save and may improve your Social Security payments. Consider your professional satisfaction, health, and personal goals to establish your desired retirement age.

Lifestyle Expectations
Your retirement lifestyle will determine your financial demands. Consider the questions below:

Where do you want to live? The cost of living differs significantly between urban, suburban, and rural areas, as well as between countries.

What activities do you intend to pursue? Hobbies, travel, and leisure activities can have a substantial impact on your finances.

What are your housing plans? Will you downsize, move, or remain in your current home? Each choice has unique financial repercussions.

Personal Financial Goals:
Setting precise financial goals is critical to a successful retirement plan. These goals may include:

Debt elimination: Aim to pay off your mortgage, loans, and credit card debt before retiring.

Maintain an emergency reserve to handle any unforeseen bills.

Healthcare savings: Set aside funds for medical needs, especially long-term care.
Consider how you wish to leave a legacy for your family or philanthropic causes.
Evaluating your current financial situation
To establish whether you are on track to meet your retirement goals, assess your present financial condition. Here's how.

Assess Your Savings and Investments

Determine the entire value of your retirement accounts, which includes 401(k), IRAs, and other investment portfolios. Estimate the long-term growth of these assets using internet tools or consulting with a financial professional.

Analyze Your Income Sources.

Identify all prospective retirement income streams, including Social Security, pensions, rental income, and part-time employment. Estimate the monthly income from each source.

Review your expenses.

Track your current spending and forecast how they may change in retirement. Consider both necessary expenses (housing, utilities, groceries) and discretionary spending (vacation, entertainment).

Actionable Steps for Visualizing Your Future Retirement

- **Step 1:** Create a retirement budget.
  Create a detailed budget, including your estimated retirement income and costs. This can help you figure out how much you need to save to maintain your chosen lifestyle.

- **Step 2:** Calculate Your Required Savings.
  Use retirement calculators to determine how much money you'll need to save. These methods take into account inflation, investment returns, and life expectancy. A general rule of thumb is to aim for retirement savings equal to 25 times your annual costs.

- **Step 3:** Set Milestones.
  Break down your savings goal into smaller, more doable benchmarks. For example, set savings goals for specific ages (e.g., $100,000 by age 40, $500,000 by age 50).

- **Step 4:** Adjust Your Plan
  Regularly assess and adapt your retirement plan to reflect changes in your financial circumstances, market conditions, and personal objectives. This helps you keep on track and may make any required changes.

- **Step 5:** Seek professional advice.
  Consider speaking with a financial expert to receive specialized advice and solutions tailored to your specific situation. They can assist you in optimizing your savings, investment, and withdrawal strategies.

Defining your retirement objectives requires careful consideration of your intended retirement age, lifestyle expectations, and personal financial goals. You may construct a strong retirement plan by assessing your present financial situation and taking practical activities to visualize your future retirement. Regularly evaluating and updating your plan can help you stay on track to meet your retirement goals.

Setting Clear, Realistic Retirement Objectives

Setting realistic retirement objectives requires a deliberate strategy that takes into account your age, lifestyle, and financial status.

Here's a step-by-step strategy for setting realistic and attainable retirement goals:

1. Assess your current financial situation.

Begin by reviewing your present financial situation.

This includes:

- **Income and Expense:** Track your monthly income and expenses to better understand your cash flow.
- **Saving and Investing:** Examine your savings accounts, retirement plans, and other investments.
- **Debts:** List all of your debts, including mortgages, loans, and credit card amounts.

2. Define your retirement lifestyle

Your preferred lifestyle will have a big impact on your retirement aspirations.

Consider:
- **Living Arrangements:** Do you intend to downsize, relocate to another city, or remain in your existing home?
- **Activities and Hobbies:** Consider what things you wish to pursue, such as travel, hobbies, or volunteering.
- **Healthcare Needs:** Consider prospective healthcare bills, particularly if you have any pre-existing problems.

3. Establish Age-Based Milestones.
Your age is a critical factor in retirement planning.

Below are some general guidelines:

In your twenties and thirties, aim to save at least one times your annual pay by age 301. Focus on accumulating an emergency fund and beginning retirement savings early.

In your 40s, strive to have three times your annual wage saved by age 40. Increase your retirement contributions while paying off high-interest bills.
- **In Your 50s:** By age 50, aim for 6 times your annual salary. Maximize your retirement account contributions,

including catch-up contributions if available.

- **In Your 60s:** Aim for 8x your annual wage by age 60. Plan for the transition to retirement, including when to begin collecting Social Security benefits.

4. Create a savings plan.

Create a savings plan based on your financial evaluation and lifestyle goals.

- **Monthly Savings Goal:** Determine how much you need to save each month to meet your retirement goals.
- **Investment strategy:** Choose an investment strategy that matches your risk tolerance and time horizon. Diversify your portfolio to ensure a balance of risk and return.

5. Monitor and adjust your plan.

Regularly assess your retirement plan to ensure you're on track.

- **Annual reviews:** Conduct an annual financial evaluation and alter your savings and investing plans as necessary.
- **Life Changes:** Be prepared to adapt your strategy in response to big life

events such as marriage, children, or work changes.

Creating attainable retirement objectives needs a thorough assessment of your financial condition, a vision for your retirement lifestyle, and a consistent savings plan. Setting age-based milestones and frequently monitoring your progress might help you plan for a secure and satisfying retirement.

How to Identify Your Ideal Retirement Lifestyle

Envisioning your retirement lifestyle is an important step in preparing for a rewarding and joyful future. Here's a thorough guide to imagining your ideal retirement, as well as a lifestyle quiz to help you identify your goals.

Where Will You Live?
Consider the finest atmosphere for your retirement years:

- **Location:** Do you prefer the serenity of the countryside, the energy of a city, or the quaintness of a coastal town? Consider the climate, accessibility to family, and access to healthcare.

- **Housing:** Decide whether you want to downsize, remain in your existing home, or relocate to a retirement community. Consider the upkeep and costs of each alternative.

What Will You Do?

Identify activities to keep you occupied and happy:

- **Hobbies & Interests:** Retirement is an excellent opportunity to pursue old passions or discover new ones. Find activities that you enjoy, such as gardening, drawing, or playing a musical instrument.
- **Travel:** If you enjoy traveling, plan visits to places you've always wanted to visit. Consider both local and foreign travel, and think about how frequently you'd like to embark on these excursions.
- **Volunteerism and community involvement:** Many retirees find fulfillment by giving back to their communities. Look for volunteer opportunities that match your interests and talents.

What Matters Most

Consider what will give you the most satisfaction and peace:

- **Relationships:** Maintaining good bonds with family and friends is critical. Plan regular visits and events, and consider moving closer to loved ones.
- **Health & Wellness:** Prioritize both your physical and mental wellness. Incorporate regular exercise, a healthy diet, and thoughtful activities into your daily routine.
- **Financial Security:** Make sure you have a good financial plan that fits your lifestyle. To keep on track, assess your finances on a regular basis, and make any necessary adjustments.

Lifestyle Questionnaire

Use this questionnaire to help establish your retirement priorities.

- Where do you envision yourself living in retirement?
  City, countryside, seaside town, or something else?
  Close to family and friends, or in a new place?

- Which sort of house do you prefer?
  Current home, smaller home, retirement community, or something else?

- What activities would you like to pursue?
  Hobbies, travel, volunteering, or any other interests?

- How important is travel for you?
  Frequent overseas trips, occasional local visits, or little travel?

- What role will family and friends have in your retirement?
  Regular visits, living locally, or sustaining long-distance relationships?

- How will you prioritize your health and well-being?
  Regular exercise, a nutritious diet, mental health habits, or something else?

- What are your financial goals for retirement?
  Maintaining present lifestyle, reducing costs, or other financial plans?

- What kind of legacy do you would like to leave?

Financial legacy, communal impact, family traditions, or anything else?

By carefully analyzing these factors and completing the questionnaire, you can build a vision for a retirement that is both attainable and emotionally rewarding.

Evaluating Your Current Financial Situation

Assessing your existing financial condition is a critical step toward financial stability and accomplishing your objectives. Here's a guide to evaluating your savings, income, and expenses, as well as a financial health checklist to help you figure out where you are right now.

Step-by-step assessment

1. Determine Your Income: Identify all sources of income, including salary, freelance work, rental income, dividends, and other sources.

- **Total monthly income:** Add up all of these sources to get a good idea of your overall monthly revenue.

2. Track Your Expenses: Categorize them. Separate your spending into categories like housing, utilities, groceries, transportation, entertainment, and miscellaneous.

- **Keep a record of your expenses:** Track all of your expenses for at least a month using a budgeting tool or a simple spreadsheet.
- **Evaluate your spending habits:** Determine where you can save money and where you need to spend more.

3. Evaluate Your Savings: Create an emergency fund to cover at least 3-6 months of living expenses.

- **Retirement savings:** Check your retirement accounts to make sure you're making regular contributions.
- **Other savings goals:** Consider saving for other goals such as a down payment on a house, education, or travel.

Checklist for Your Financial Health

1. Income Stability: Do you have a consistent and dependable source of income?
- Are you diversifying your revenue streams?

2. Expense Management: - Do you track your expenses regularly?
- Do you keep to a budget?

3. Savings and Investments: - Do you have an emergency fund to cover 3-6 months of expenses?
- Are you saving at least 20% of your earnings?
- Do you plan on making long-term investments?

4. Debt Management: Do you efficiently manage your debt?
- Is your debt to income ratio less than 36%?

5. Insurance Coverage: - Do you have enough health, life, and property insurance?

6. Credit Health: Do you regularly check your credit report?
- Is your credit score in a good range?

7. Financial Goals: - Have you established short and long-term financial objectives?
- Do you keep track of and alter your goals on a regular basis?

8. Estate Planning: Do you have a will or estate plan in place?

By following these steps and using the checklist, you can acquire a thorough picture of your financial situation and take aggressive efforts to improve it. Regularly assessing and updating your financial plan will keep you on track to meet your financial objectives.

Chapter 2:

Building Your Retirement Income

Building your retirement income requires careful planning and effective resource management to achieve financial security in your later years.

Here are some important steps to consider:

1. Determine Your Needs: Begin by evaluating your retirement expenses. Consider your lifestyle, healthcare expenses, and any planned trips or hobbies. This will offer you an accurate view of how much income you'll require.

2. Diversify Your Income: Relying on one source of income might be dangerous. Diversify your income sources by mixing Social Security benefits, pensions, savings, investments, and even part-time work. This method can result in more consistent and reliable revenue.

3. Invest wisely: Make a balanced investment portfolio consisting of stocks, bonds, and other assets. This can help to mitigate risk and ensure growth. As you approach retirement, gradually transition to more conservative investments to protect your assets.

4. Use Tax-Advantaged funds: Take advantage of tax-advantaged retirement funds such as IRAs and 401(k). These accounts provide tax benefits, allowing your money to grow more efficiently. Consider both standard and Roth choices to spread your tax burden.

5. Develop a Withdrawal Strategy: Determine how you will withdraw funds from your retirement accounts. The 4% rule advocates taking 4% of your retirement funds annually. Adjust this technique to meet your needs and market conditions.

6. Manage Debt: Going into retirement with little debt can greatly minimize your financial load. Pay off high-interest bills and avoid incurring additional debt as you near retirement.

7. Stay Informed and Flexible: Monitor changes in the economy, tax laws, and investment opportunities. Prepare to change your plan as needed to stay on target.

Following these steps, you can create a strong retirement income plan that supports a comfortable and secure retirement.

The Foundations of a Retirement Income Strategy

Retirement income sources are critical for maintaining financial security and comfort in your later years.

Here are a few common types:

- **Social Security:** This government-provided payment is calculated based on your earnings history and offers a consistent income stream. It is a critical component of many seniors' income strategies.
  Pensions are employer-sponsored schemes that offer regular income upon retirement. They are becoming less prevalent, yet they continue to provide a significant source of income for many.

Personal investments include stocks, bonds, mutual funds, and real estate. These assets may generate dividends, interest, and rental income.

- **Retirement Accounts:** Accounts such as 401(k), IRAs, and Roth IRAs allow you to save and invest for retirement while benefiting from tax advantages. Annuities are insurance contracts that promise an income stream for the rest of one's life or for a certain length of time.
- **Part-time Work:** Many retirees prefer to work part-time to augment their income and stay active.

The importance of diversifying income sources

Diversifying your retirement income sources is important for a variety of reasons:

- **Risk Mitigation:** Depending solely on one source of income might be problematic. If that source fails or underperforms, it may risk your financial stability. Diversification spreads risk across several streams.
- **Inflation Protection:** Different income sources respond differently to inflation. For example, Social Security

benefits are indexed for inflation, whereas fixed pensions are not. A combination can help defend against the destabilizing consequences of inflation.

- **Market Volatility:** Stock market investments are subject to volatility. You can keep your income steady even during market downturns if you have other sources of income, such as Social Security or annuities.
- **Longevity Risk:** As people live longer lives, they are more likely to outlive their savings.

Diversified income streams might provide a more consistent income over the long term.

Examples of Retirement Income Strategies:
- **The Bucket Strategy:** Divide your assets into three "buckets" based on when you will need the money. The first bucket is for immediate needs (1-2 years), the second is for medium-term needs (3-10 years), and the third is for long-term needs (10 years or more). This method reduces risk and ensures liquidity.

- **The Four Percent Rule:** This strategy proposes withdrawing 4% of your retirement savings each year, adjusted for inflation. This strategy seeks to stretch your money for at least 30 years.
- **Income Floor:** This technique entails ensuring that your necessary expenses are covered by reliable income sources such as Social Security, pensions, and annuities. Any additional costs can be offset by more variable sources, such as investments.

Understanding and adopting these techniques can help you build a strong and durable retirement income strategy that supports your preferred lifestyle.

Exploring Social Security: Timing and Benefits

Social Security is a government program that offers financial help to pensioners, disabled people, and the survivors of dead workers. The benefits are paid by payroll taxes collected under the Federal Insurance Contributions Act (FICA).
Below is an explanation of how it works:

- **Eligibility:** To be eligible for Social Security benefits, you must have earned at least 40 credits, which is roughly equivalent to 10 years of labor.
- **Benefit Calculation:** Your benefits are determined using your 35 highest-earning years. If you have less than 35 years of earnings, zeros are averaged in.
- **Full Retirement Age (FRA):** This is the age when you can get full Social Security benefits. Most people's ages range from 66 to 67, depending on their birth year.

When to Claim Benefits for Maximum Payouts?

- **Early Retirement:** You can begin claiming benefits as early as age 62, but your monthly benefit will be reduced by approximately 25-30% compared to your FRA payout.
- **Full Retirement Age (FRA):** Claiming at your FRA guarantees you receive the full benefit amount.
- **Delayed Retirement:** If you wait to claim benefits after your FRA, your payout will grow by approximately 8% per year until you reach the age of 70.

This may result in a much bigger monthly benefit.

The Impact of Early vs. Delayed Benefits

- **Early Benefits:** If you claim early, your monthly payment will be permanently reduced. This may be appropriate if you require the income immediately or have a lower life expectancy.
- **Delayed Benefits:** Delaying benefits raises your monthly payout, which might be beneficial if you plan to live a longer life and want to optimize your lifetime benefits.

Timeline Chart for Social Security Claiming Strategies

Here's a simplified timeline to show the influence of various claiming ages:

Table

Age	Monthly Benefit (as % of FRA)	Strategy
62	~70-75%	Early Claiming
66-67	100%	Full Retirement Age
100	~124-132%	Delayed Claiming

Examples of Claiming Strategies

- **Claim Early:** If you claim at age 62, your compensation is lowered, but you will get payments for a longer period of time.
- **Claim at FRA:** Claiming at your FRA assures that you receive the full benefit amount with no reductions or increases.
- **Delay until 70:** Delaying until 70 increases your monthly payment, which can be useful if you have a longer life expectancy.

Key Considerations

- **Health and longevity:** Consider your health and family history before selecting when to file a claim.
- **Financial Needs:** Consider your immediate financial needs versus the long-term rewards.
- **Spousal Benefits:** If you are married, coordinating with your spouse's benefits will help you maximize your joint income.

Understanding these characteristics allows you to make informed decisions about when to claim Social Security based on your financial status and retirement plans.

Pension Plans: Maximizing Employer Contributions

A pension is a retirement plan in which an employer contributes to a pool of cash designated for an employee's future benefit. These funds are invested on the employee's behalf, and the earnings provide income for the employee after retirement.

Pension Types:
1. Defined Benefit Plans.

- **Description:** These plans guarantee a certain monthly payment at retirement, which is often based on salary and years of service.
- **Pros:** Consistent income, often adjusted for inflation.
- **Cons:** Less flexible, and benefits are contingent on the employer's financial stability.

2. Defined Contribution Plans.
Employees contribute a defined amount or percentage of their wages to fund their retirement accounts. Employers frequently match employee contributions up to a particular amount.

- **Pros:** More control over investments, with the potential for larger returns.
- **Cons:** Retirement income is based on investment performance, which might be unpredictable.

Tips for Maximizing Employer Contributions

- **Contribute Enough to Receive the Full Match:** Make sure you contribute the minimum amount required to receive the full employer match. This is basically free money deposited into your retirement account.

- **Start early:** The sooner you begin contributing, the longer your money has to grow through compound interest.
- **Increase Contributions Gradually:** If you can't afford to max out your contributions right now, gradually increase them over time, especially as you receive increases or bonuses.
- **Stay till you're vested:** Vesting refers to the amount of time you must work for your employer before you are fully entitled to the company's payments. Make sure you understand your plan's vesting period and aim to stay until you are completely vested.

Pension Rollover Options

When you change employment or retire, you may want to explore rolling over your pension to another retirement plan.

Here are a few choices:

Traditional IRAs provide for tax-deferred growth of your investments.

- **Roth IRAs:** Contributions are made after taxes, but withdrawals are tax-free in retirement.
- **401(k):** If your new job allows it, you can roll your pension into their 401(k).
- **Annuity:** Offers a guaranteed income stream, which can be useful for those looking for a consistent, predictable income.

When considering a rollover, it's crucial to understand the tax implications and ensure that the new account matches your retirement goals.

Building a Personal Retirement Portfolio

Building a retirement portfolio requires careful planning to balance growth, income, and risk management.
Here's a guide to help you design a personalized investment portfolio:

Asset Allocation:
Asset allocation is the process of splitting your investments into several asset classes, such as stocks, bonds, and cash. The right combination

is determined by your risk tolerance, time horizon, and retirement objectives.

Stocks have bigger potential rewards but also carry a higher risk. Ideal for long-term growth.
Bonds offer more steady returns and lower risk. Excellent for income and capital preservation.
Cash provides liquidity and protection, but yields modest returns. Suitable for short-term needs and emergencies.

Risk Tolerance
Risk tolerance refers to your capacity and readiness to withstand market volatility. It is determined by factors such as your financial condition, investment experience, and emotional tolerance for risk.

High risk tolerance means more equities and fewer bonds. Suitable for younger investors with longer time horizons.
Moderate risk tolerance: A balanced portfolio of equities and bonds. Ideal for midcareer investors.
Low risk tolerance means investing more in bonds and cash and less in stocks. Suitable for people approaching or in retirement.

Rebalancing Strategies

Rebalancing means modifying your portfolio to keep your intended asset allocation. This can help you control risk and keep your portfolio on track with your goals.

Periodic rebalancing involves adjusting your portfolio at regular intervals (e.g., annually). Threshold rebalancing occurs when your asset allocation deviates by a particular percentage from your target.

Combination Approach: To keep on track, use periodic and threshold rebalancing.

Sample Portfolios for Retirement Timelines

Early Career (20 to 35 years)
Stocks: 80 percent
Bonds: 15%.
Cash: 5%

Mid-Career (35-50 Years)
Stocks: 60%
Bonds: 30%.
Cash: 10%

Pre-retirement (50–65 years)
Stocks: 40%

Bonds: 50%.
Cash: 10%

Retirement (65+ years)
Stock: 30%.
Bonds: 60%
Cash: 10%

Tips for Success

- **Start Early:** The earlier you start investing, the greater the likelihood that your funds will grow over time.
- **Stay Diversified:** To reduce risk, spread your investments across multiple asset classes.
- **Monitor and Adjust:** Review your portfolio on a regular basis and make any necessary modifications.

Following these rules, you can design a strong investment portfolio that supports your retirement goals and adjusts to your changing needs over time.

Chapter 3:

Risk Management in Retirement

Risk management in retirement is critical for achieving financial stability and peace of mind in one's golden years. It entails recognizing, assessing, and minimizing various risks that may jeopardize a person's financial stability and general well-being.

Here are some important factors and solutions for effective retirement risk management:

1. Market Risk.
Market risk is the likelihood that investment returns will fluctuate owing to economic conditions, political events, or other factors. This volatility can have a severe influence on retirement savings and overall financial stability. Retirees can manage market risk by diversifying their investment portfolios among asset classes such as stocks, bonds, and cash. Investing in low-cost, passive investment vehicles such as index funds or

exchange-traded funds (ETFs) can also help to mitigate the effects of market volatility.

2. Inflation Risk

Inflation risk is the possible reduction in the buying power of retirement savings as prices rise over time. Inflation can diminish the value of fixed-income investments and the real income generated by retirement assets. To mitigate inflation risk, retirees might incorporate inflation-protected investments into their portfolios, such as Treasury Inflation-Protected Securities (TIPS) or inflation-adjusted annuities. Maintaining a portion of your investments in growth assets, such as stocks, can also help to mitigate the consequences of inflation.

3. Longevity Risk.

Longevity risk refers to the risk of outliving one's retirement resources. This risk has grown in significance as life expectancies have increased. To reduce longevity risk, retirees might consider purchasing annuities that give a guaranteed income for life. Furthermore, using a cautious withdrawal strategy, such as the 4% rule, can help ensure that your funds endure throughout retirement.

4. Healthcare Costs.

Healthcare bills can be a considerable hardship in retirement, particularly given the escalating costs of medical treatment and long-term care. To mitigate this risk, retirees might consider acquiring long-term care insurance and, if qualified, contributing to a health savings account (HSA). Additionally, budgeting for anticipated healthcare expenses in the retirement budget is critical.

5. Unexpected expenses

Unexpected expenses, such as house maintenance or family emergencies, might derail a retiree's financial plans. To plan for them, retirees should have an emergency fund with enough liquidity to cover unexpected expenses. This fund should be conveniently available and not tied down to long-term investments.

Effective risk management in retirement necessitates a comprehensive approach that covers a variety of financial issues. Diversifying investments, planning for inflation and healthcare costs, and preparing for unforeseen expenses can help retirees secure their financial resources and maintain their preferred lifestyle throughout retirement.

Evaluating Market Risks: Stocks, Bonds, and Diversification

Market risk, also known as systemic risk, refers to the possibility of investors losing money as a result of factors affecting financial market performance in general. Diversification cannot reduce this form of risk, which is inherent in all market-related investments. Market risk can come from a variety of causes, including economic downturns, political instability, interest rate fluctuations, and natural calamities.

Market risk has a big impact on seniors' financial security. Because retirees sometimes rely on their financial portfolios for income, market downturns can devalue their assets, potentially resulting in a lower quality of living. Furthermore, retirees may have less time to recover from market losses than younger investors, so it is critical to handle this risk wisely.

Diversifying Investments to Reduce Risk.

Diversification is a risk-reduction technique that involves spreading investments over many asset classes, industries, and geographical areas. The theory is that by diversifying your investments, the poor performance of one can be offset by the higher performance of another, resulting in a more consistent overall return.

Here are some basic steps to diversify your investments:

- **Invest in a variety of asset classes:** Include stocks, bonds, real estate, and cash equivalents in your portfolio. Each asset class responds differently in different market conditions, which helps to balance risk.
- **Diversify Within Asset Classes:** For example, invest in equities from various industries such as technology, healthcare, and consumer goods. Similarly, bonds might be classified as government, corporate, or municipal.
- **Geographical Diversity:** Invest in both domestic and international markets to diversify risk across economic regions.
- **Use of Mutual Funds and ETFs:** These investment vehicles provide

diversity by combining funds from multiple participants to purchase a diverse variety of securities.

Examples of Portfolio Diversification for various Risk Tolerances

Conservative portfolio:
60% of bonds are government or high-quality corporate bonds.
20% Stocks are large-cap, dividend-paying stocks.
10% Real Estate: Real Estate Investment Trusts (REITs).
10% cash equivalents include money market funds and short-term certificates of deposit (CDs).

A moderate portfolio consists of 40% bonds, including both government and corporate bonds.

- **40% Stocks:** A balanced portfolio of large-cap, mid-cap, and international stocks.
- **10% real estate:** REITs.
- Commodities or hedge funds account for 10% of alternative investments.

- **Aggressive Portfolio:** 20% Bonds: Mostly corporate bonds with strong returns.
- **60% Stocks:** A varied portfolio of large-cap, mid-cap, small-cap, and international stocks.
- **10% real estate:** REITs. Commodities, private equity, and venture capital account for 10% of the alternatives.

By adjusting asset allocation to individual risk tolerance, retirees can better manage market risk and achieve a more stable financial future.

Managing Longevity Risk: Ensuring Your Income Lasts

Longevity risk is the probability that you will outlive your retirement resources. As life expectancy rises, this risk becomes more important, necessitating cautious preparation to assure financial security in retirement.

Strategies for Mitigating Longevity Risk Delay Social Security payments: By delaying Social Security payments until age 70, retirees can increase their monthly payouts.

Annuities: Purchasing annuities can provide a guaranteed lifetime income stream, ensuring that retirees do not outlive their resources.

Diversified Investments: Having a diverse investment portfolio that includes growth assets will help you sustain income over time.

The 4% Rule advocates withdrawing 4% of your retirement assets each year, adjusted for inflation, to help ensure that your savings last.

Long-term Care Insurance: This can assist cover medical expenses in later life, reducing the financial strain on retirement resources.

Life Expectancy and Income Annuities

Life expectancy estimations are critical in retirement planning. They help calculate how long your funds should endure. A variety of factors influence life expectancy, including age, gender, lifestyle, and family medical history. Tools such as the Annuity.org Life Expectancy Calculator can provide tailored estimations.

Income annuities are financial instruments that pay you regular payments for the rest of your life or for a certain length of time. They can be an effective technique for mitigating longevity risk by providing a consistent income source. Immediate annuities begin payments almost immediately following a lump sum investment, whereas delayed annuities begin payments at a later date.

Longevity Risk Checklist

Here's a checklist for managing longevity risk:

- **Estimate Life Expectancy:** Using tools and calculators, you may acquire a personalized estimate of your life span.
- **Maximize Savings:** Make the maximum contribution to retirement accounts and examine other savings options.
- **Delay Social Security:** Consider delaying Social Security benefits in order to maximize monthly payouts.
- **Consider Annuities:** Compare several forms of annuities that give guaranteed income.
- **Diversify Your Investments:** Maintain a balanced portfolio that includes growth assets.
- **Healthcare Costs:** Incorporate long-term care insurance into your retirement strategy.

Review your retirement plan on a regular basis and make any necessary adjustments to stay on track.

Following these tactics and evaluating your plan on a regular basis will help you manage longevity risk and ensure a financially secure retirement.

Inflation: How to Plan for Rising Costs in Retirement

Inflation reduces the purchasing power of money over time, so the same amount of money buys fewer goods and services as prices rise. This can have a substantial impact on retirees, particularly those on fixed incomes or with savings that are not adjusted for inflation. For example, if inflation averages 3% per year, a retiree's savings can lose nearly half their purchasing power over 25 years.

Historical Inflation Data
To understand the impact, consider some historical data:

In 1923, a loaf of bread cost $0.09, a gallon of milk $0.56, and a new vehicle $380.

2023: The same things cost $3.68, $4.21, and $48,182, respectively.

This sharp rise in prices demonstrates how inflation can erode purchasing power over time. For retirees, this implies that their funds must increase to keep up with rising prices.

Tips to Protect Against Inflation

Here are some techniques to help prevent inflation:

Invest in stocks: Stocks have typically surpassed inflation in the long run. Consider a diverse portfolio with a variety of equities to help you develop your savings.

Treasury Inflation-Protected Securities (TIPS) are government bonds meant to safeguard against inflation. TIPS' main value rises with inflation, serving as a hedge against rising prices.

Real estate investments, such as **Real Estate Investment Trusts (REITs)**, can generate income and potential gain that outpaces inflation.

Commodities: Investing in commodities such as gold and oil can also provide a hedge against inflation, as their prices tend to rise when inflation increases.

High-Yield Savings Accounts: While not a full answer, putting some money in high-yield savings accounts can help offset the impact of inflation on cash holdings.

How Inflation Affected Retirees in the Past

Inflation has had a significant influence on pensioners, especially during times of severe inflation. For example, throughout the 1970s and early 1980s, inflation rates in the United States reached double digits, severely reducing the value of fixed incomes and savings. More recently, the 2022 inflation rise, which reached 9.1%, has put a pressure on seniors' budgets.

Retirees frequently confront rising healthcare, housing, and other expenditures, making it critical to have an inflation strategy in place. By adding inflation-protected investments and evaluating their financial plans on a regular basis, retirees can better protect their purchasing power and standard of living.

Chapter 4:

Retirement Income Styles

Retirement income styles are the numerous techniques retirees might take to create money throughout their retirement years. Individual preferences, risk tolerance, financial goals, and the desire for stability over development all have an impact on these types.

Here are several popular retirement income styles:

1. Systematic Withdrawal Plan (SWP).
A Systematic Withdrawal Plan entails consistently withdrawing a set percentage or amount from retirement funds. This technique gives you more freedom and control over your investments, but it takes careful planning to prevent emptying assets too soon. The 4% rule is a popular guideline that suggests retirees withdraw 4% of their portfolio each year, adjusted for inflation.

2) Annuities

Annuities are types of insurance that promise income for the rest of one's life or for a set length of time. They can be immediate, commencing very immediately after a lump-sum investment, or deferred, beginning at a later date. Annuities provide stability and peace of mind, generating a consistent income source regardless of market conditions.

3. Bucket Strategy.

The Bucket Strategy categorizes retirement funds into "buckets" based on time horizon and risk degree. Typically, there are three categories: short-term (cash and bonds for urgent needs), medium-term (balanced investments over the following 5-10 years), and long-term (growth stocks). This technique reduces risk and assures liquidity for urgent expenses while still allowing for growth.

4. Dividend Investing.

Dividend investing aims to establish a portfolio of dividend-paying equities. These stocks generate regular income in the form of dividends, which can be reinvested or used for living expenditures. This strategy has the potential to generate income and capital appreciation, but it is subject to market risk.

5. Bond Laddering

Bond laddering entails purchasing bonds of various maturities. As each bond matures, the principal is reinvested in a new bond at the bottom of the ladder. This technique generates consistent income while reducing interest rate risk by distributing investments over multiple maturities.

6. Real Estate Income.

Investing in real estate, such as rental properties or Real Estate Investment Trusts (REITs), can generate a consistent income stream through rental payments or dividends. Real estate can also provide potential appreciation, but it requires active management and carries market and liquidity risks.

7. Part-time work.

Some retirees continue to work part-time to supplement their retirement income. This can provide additional financial stability while keeping retirees engaged and active. However, it may not be appropriate for everyone, depending on their health and personal preferences.

Individual variables, such as financial objectives, risk tolerance, and lifestyle preferences, influence which retirement income type is best for you. A mix of these tactics can provide a more balanced approach, ensuring a consistent income while mitigating risk. Regularly assessing and updating the retirement plan is essential for adapting to changing needs and market conditions.

Income-Focused vs. Growth-Focused: Which Style Fits You?

Income-Driven Investment Strategy:

- **Objective:** To provide a consistent source of income from dividends, interest, or other forms of investment income.
- Typical investments include dividend-paying equities, bonds, real estate investment trusts (REITs), and other income-producing assets.
- **Risk Level:** Generally less risky than growth-oriented programs, but

nevertheless vulnerable to market swings and interest rate adjustments.
- **Ideal for:** Investors wanting regular income, such as retirees or those who require continuous cash flow.

Growth-Driven Investment Strategy:

- **Goal:** Increase capital appreciation by investing in companies with high growth potential.
- Typical investments include equities in companies that are predicted to develop faster than the average, as well as technology stocks and other high-growth industries.
- **Risk Level:** High risk owing to the possibility of considerable price fluctuation.
- **Ideal for:** Long-term investors with a high risk tolerance who want to see their investment value develop significantly.

Assessing Your Risk Tolerance and Goals

To establish which investing strategy is best for you, examine the following:

- **Low risk tolerance:** Low risk tolerance indicates a preference for stability and predictability. Income-focused techniques might be more appropriate.
- **High risk tolerance:** Willing to accept market volatility and probable losses in exchange for higher profits. Growth-focused tactics may be a better fit.

Investment Goals:
- **Short-term Goals:** Need money within a few years. Income-oriented investments can deliver consistent returns.
- **Long-Term Goals:** Seeking to increase wealth over a longer period. Growth-oriented investments have larger potential returns.

Income Needs:
- **Regular money Requirement:** If you require continuous money, an income-focused plan is best.
- **Wealth Accumulation:** If you want to accumulate wealth, a growth-oriented strategy may be more suitable.

Sample Retirement Income Strategies for;
Income-Driven Investors:

Bucket Strategy:
- **Bucket 1:** Set aside 1-2 years' worth of living costs in a high-yield savings account for liquidity.
- **Bucket 2:** Invest in bonds or CDs for medium-term needs (3-10 years).
- **Bucket 3:** Invest the remaining cash in dividend-paying equities and REITs for long-term income.

Systematic withdrawals:
Withdraw a fixed percentage (e.g., 4%) of your portfolio each year, adjusted for inflation.

- **For growth-oriented investors:**
  The Total Return Strategy involves investing in a diverse portfolio of growth stocks and reinvesting dividends and capital gains to maximize growth.
  Periodically adjust the portfolio to maintain the appropriate asset allocation.

- **Hybrid Approach:**

Combine growth and income investments. For example, set aside a chunk for high-growth stocks and another for dividend-paying stocks.

Understanding your risk tolerance and investment goals allows you to select the approach that best meets your financial needs and retirement plans.

Balancing Risks: Understanding Your Financial Mindset

Understanding your financial thinking is critical to making sound investing decisions. Here are some crucial features that help you determine your financial personality:

Risk-Taker:
- **Characteristics:** Comfortable with uncertainty, eager to take risks for larger profits, and not easily fazed by market volatility.
- **Investment Style:** Favors growth-oriented investments, such as stocks in emerging markets or technology sectors.

Characteristics of a risk-averse investor include a preference for stability and security, avoidance of high-risk investments, and emphasis on wealth preservation.

- **Investment Style**: Prefers income-producing investments like bonds, dividend-paying equities, and real estate.

Balanced:

- **Characteristics:** Seeks a balance of growth and stability, and is willing to assume moderate risks in exchange for balanced returns.
- **Investment Style:** Balances growth and income investments to create a diverse portfolio.

Strategies to Balance Risk and Reward in Retirement

To limit risk, diversify your investments across asset types (e.g., stocks, bonds, and real estate). Diversify across asset classes (e.g., across sectors and locations) to reduce risk.

Allocate your portfolio depending on age, risk tolerance, and retirement goals.
A typical rule of thumb is to subtract your age from 100 to calculate the amount of your portfolio that should be allocated to equities.

Regular rebalancing involves reviewing and adjusting your portfolio to maintain the correct asset allocation.
Rebalancing reduces risk and ensures that your assets are aligned with your objectives.

Include income-generating assets, such as dividend-paying equities, bonds, and REITs, to ensure consistent cash flow.
Consider annuities if you want guaranteed income in retirement.

Financial Personality Quiz
Take this quiz to determine your financial mindset:

How do you feel about the market volatility?
- A. Excited about the prospect for high profits.
- B. Anxious, preferring stability.
- C. Accept it as part of investment, but take a balanced approach.

What is your major investment objective?

- A. Ensuring maximum growth and financial appreciation.
- B. Generating consistent income while conserving capital.
- C. Creating a balance of growth and revenue.

How would you react to a 20% reduction in your portfolio's value?

- A. Consider it a buying opportunity.
- B. Consider selling to prevent more losses.
- C. Assess and rebalance your portfolio.

What is your investing horizon?

- A. Long-term (more than 10 years).
- B. Short-term (1 to 5 years).
- C. Medium-term (5 to 10 years).

How much investing experience do you have?

- A. Extensive experience with difficult investments.
- B. Limited, preferring simple and reliable investments.

- C. Moderate; knowledgeable with a variety of financial alternatives.

Results:

- **Mostly A's:** You are a risk-taker. Consider a growth-oriented investing plan.
- **Mostly B's:** You are risk-averse. An income-focused investment strategy may be the best fit for you.
- **Mostly C's:** You have a balanced perspective. A diversified portfolio that includes both growth and income investments is excellent.

Understanding your financial personality enables you to design your investing strategy to successfully balance risk and reward, resulting in a comfortable and secure retirement.

The Retirement Income Style Matrix

The Retirement Income Style Matrix (RISA®) is a tool that helps retirees determine their preferred method of producing income in retirement. Professor Wade Pfau and Alex Murguia developed the matrix, which categorizes retirement income strategies based on two main dimensions:

Safety First Versus Probability-Based:

- **Safety First:** Prioritizes assured income streams like annuities and pensions.
- **Probability-Based:** Relies on investment growth and periodic withdrawals, allowing for some income unpredictability.

Optionality versus Commitment:

- **Optionality:** Values flexibility and the capacity to change techniques over time.
- **Commitment:** Seeking a permanent, dependable source of retirement income.
- Understanding where you lie along these dimensions allows you to select a retirement income strategy that matches your tastes and comfort level.

How To Use the RISA® Matrix

- **Assess your preferences:** Determine whether you value guaranteed income (Safety First) or prefer market-based income (Probability Based).

- Determine whether you prefer flexibility (optionality) or a steady, long-term plan (commitment).
- **Identify your style:** Determine where you fit within the matrix based on your choices. This can help you determine which retirement income strategies are best for you.
- **Implement your strategy:** Use the matrix's insights to choose and implement a retirement income strategy that suits your needs.

Case Studies
- **Case Study 1:** Safety First plus Commitment

  John, 65, is a recent retiree who avoids risk and prefers stability.

  - **Strategy:** John chooses a fixed annuity, which guarantees a monthly income for life. This gives him a steady income without having to worry about market volatility.

- **Case Study 2:** Probability-Based + Optionality

Sarah, 60, continues to work, is OK with market risk, and enjoys flexibility.

- **Strategy:** Sarah's investment strategy is to diversify her portfolio with both growth stocks and bonds. She intends to remove a portion of her capital each year, changing her strategy according to market conditions and her requirements.

- **Case Study 3:** Safety First + Optionality

  Michael, 70, is retired and seeks a guaranteed income with some flexibility.

  - **Strategy:** Michael's strategy combines a fixed annuity for basic living needs with a bond ladder for additional income. This strategy ensures stability while allowing for considerable flexibility over time.

- **Case Study #4:** Probability-Based + Commitment

  Emily, 62, is semi-retired and comfortable with investing risk. She prefers a long-term plan.

  - **Strategy:** Emily invests in a balanced portfolio of stocks and bonds and follows a systematic withdrawal strategy. She is committed to this strategy, believing in the long-term growth potential of her investments.

Tools for Assessing Your Fit inside the Matrix
RISA® Questionnaire:
Take the RISA® examination to determine your retirement income style. This 15-minute assessment assesses your choices and assigns you to a specific box on the matrix.

Financial Advisor Consultation:
Consult a financial counselor to discuss your preferences and create a personalized retirement income plan.
- **Self-Assessment:** Consider your risk tolerance, income needs, and flexibility

preferences. Use the matrix to aid in your decision-making process.

The Retirement Income Style Matrix can help you better understand your financial preferences and select a retirement income strategy that is appropriate for your goals and comfort level.

Chapter 5:

The Funded Ratio Methodology

The Funded Ratio Methodology compares assets and liabilities to determine the long-term viability of retirement programs. This method is especially beneficial for retirees and financial planners in determining whether an individual's resources are adequate to pay future needs.

To determine the funded ratio, divide the total value of assets by the total amount of liabilities. The formula is: Funded Ratio = Total Liabilities / Total Assets.

- **Assets:** This includes all retirement savings, investments, and other financial resources accessible for retirement.
- **Liabilities:** Indicate the present value of any future retirement expenses, such

as living expenses, healthcare, and other projected expenditures.

Interpreting the funded ratio:

A funded ratio greater than one indicates that assets surpass liabilities, implying that the individual is well prepared for retirement. A higher ratio indicates better financial security and the possibility of increased expenditure or new investments in annuities or other income-generating assets.

A Funded Ratio < 1 indicates a gap where liabilities exceed assets. To reach retirement goals, you must make changes such as raising savings, lowering expenses, or taking on more investment risk.

Calculating the funded ratio requires taking into account the present value of future obligations and the discount rate. This entails applying a suitable discount rate to future expenses in order to calculate their present value. The discount rate represents the temporal value of money, taking into account factors such as inflation and investment returns.

Applications:

- **Retirement Planning:** The funded ratio provides an accurate picture of financial readiness for retirement. It enables retirees and advisors to make informed decisions regarding spending, saving, and investing.

- **Adjusting measures:** If the funded ratio is less than one, individuals might consider measures to improve their financial situation, such as deferring retirement, boosting contributions to retirement accounts, or adjusting their investment portfolio to achieve higher returns.

- **Monitoring Progress:** Calculating the funded ratio on a regular basis allows retirees to monitor their financial health over time and make adjustments as needed to keep on pace with their retirement goals.

Consider a retiree with $800,000 in retirement assets and $700,000 in predicted costs (present value). The funding ratio would be: Funded ratio: 700,000/800,000 = 1.14.

This ratio suggests that the retiree's assets are more than sufficient to cover future liabilities, implying a secure financial position for retirement.

The funded ratio methodology is an effective tool for determining retirement preparation, making financial decisions, and maintaining long-term financial security. Regular assessments and modifications based on this parameter can assist retirees in achieving their desired lifestyle and peace of mind during retirement.

What Is the Funded Ratio and Why It Matters

The funded ratio is a financial statistic that compares the value of your assets and liabilities to determine your retirement preparation. It is determined by dividing your entire assets by your total liabilities. If the ratio is more than one, it means that your assets are sufficient to meet your responsibilities, implying that you are on course for a comfortable retirement. A ratio less than 1 indicates that you may need to change your savings or expenditures to fulfill your retirement objectives.

Importance of Retirement Planning.
The funded ratio is important because it provides an overview of your financial situation and helps you determine whether you have enough resources to maintain your preferred lifestyle in retirement. It guides your savings, spending, and investment decisions, ensuring that you can fulfill future financial responsibilities without running out of money.

Real-life Examples

Example 1: Overfunding Scenario

- **Situation:** Jane has $1,200,000 in assets and a $1,000,000 estimated retirement liability.
  The funded ratio is 1,000,000/1,200,000, which equals 1.2.

- **Implication:** Jane's funded ratio of 1.2 suggests that she has more than enough assets to meet her liabilities. She can plan to retire comfortably, possibly increasing her spending or investing in annuities to ensure a regular income stream.

Example 2: Underfunding Scenario

- **Situation:** John has $800,000 in assets and a $1,000,000 estimated retirement liability.
  Funded Ratio: 1,000,000/800,000 = 0.8.

- **Implication:** John's funded ratio of 0.8 indicates that he should either raise his savings, lower his future expenditure, or take on additional investment risk to better his financial situation before retiring.

Example 3: Borderline Scenario.

- **Situation:** Mary has $950,000 in assets and $1,000,000 in estimated retirement liabilities.
  Funded Ratio: 1,000,000/950,000 = 0.95.

- **Implication:** Mary's funded ratio of 0.95 is close to one, indicating that she is on track but may need to make slight changes to her savings or spending plans to ensure a comfortable retirement.

Understanding and routinely monitoring your funded ratio will help you make informed decisions and changes to ensure a financially comfortable retirement.

Calculating Your Funded Ratio: Step-by-Step

Here's a step-by-step method for determining a funded ratio, as well as a basic calculator template to utilize.

Step-by-Step Guide to Calculating Funded Ratios

- **Determine total assets:**
  Include all retirement accounts (such as 401(k)s and IRAs), savings, investments, real estate, and other assets that can be utilized to fund your retirement.

- **Estimate total liabilities:**
  Compute all future expenses and obligations in retirement. This covers living expenses, healthcare costs, taxes, and any other planned expenses.

Calculate the funded ratio:
Apply the formula: Funded Ratio = Total Liabilities / Total Assets.

- **Example Calculation:**

    Total assets: $1,000,000.
    Total Liabilities: $900,000.
    Funded   ratio:
    900,000/1,000,000 = 1.11.

This funded ratio of 1.11 indicates that you have 111% of the assets required to pay your responsibilities, implying that you are well prepared for retirement.

Funded Ratio Calculator Template.

Table

Description	Amount
Total Assets	
- Retirement Accounts - Savings - Investments - Real Estate - Other Assets	$ $ $ $ $
Total Liabilities	
- Living Expenses - Healthcare Costs - Taxes - Other Expenses	$ $ $ $
Funded Ratio	
Funded Ratio Calculation	Funded Ratio = Total Liabilities / Total Assets.

To calculate your funded ratio, simply enter the quantities that apply to your individual scenario.

Using the Funded Ratio to Evaluate Your Readiness for Retirement

Interpreting your funded ratio is critical to determining your retirement readiness. Here's a guide to help you analyze your results and take appropriate decisions based on your funded ratio score:

Interpreting your funded ratio.
Funded Ratio: > 1

- **Interpretation:** You have more assets than liabilities, indicating that you are financially prepared for retirement.
- **Actions:**
  - **Maintain:** Continue with your present saving and investment strategies.
  - **Review:** Make sure your financial strategy is still on track with your goals.

Consider exploring opportunities for improving your retirement lifestyle or making charity contributions.

Funded Ratio: 1

- **Interpretation:** Your assets are exactly equal to your liabilities, indicating that you are on schedule for retirement.
- **Actions:**
  - **Monitor:** Pay close attention to your costs and investment performance.
    Make modest modifications to your savings or spending as needed to preserve equilibrium.
  - **Plan:** Make sure you have a backup plan for unexpected expenses.

Funded Ratio < 1.

- **Interpretation:** Your liabilities surpass your assets, indicating that you should take steps to improve your retirement readiness.
- **Actions:**
  - **Increase Savings:** Increase your retirement contributions to accumulate more assets.
  - **Reduce Expenses:** Cut back on discretionary spending to reduce your future liabilities.
  - **Reevaluate Your Investments:** Consider more

aggressive investment techniques to potentially boost returns.

- **Delay Retirement:** Put off retirement to give yourself more time to save and develop your investments.
- **Seek Advice:** A financial advisor can help you develop personalized methods to boost your funded ratio.

Example Scenario:

- **Overfunded (financed Ratio > 1):** Jane has a financed ratio of 1.2. She can continue living her existing lifestyle, explore early retirement, or perhaps boost her expenditures on hobbies and travel.
- **On Track Scenario (Funded Ratio = 1):** Mary has a funded ratio of 1. She should continue to review her financial plan and make minor adjustments as needed to stay on target.
- **Underfunded Scenario (financed Ratio < 1):** John has a financed ratio of 0.8. To improve his financial situation, he should boost his savings rate, cut his expected retirement spending, or work for a few more years.

Regularly assessing and modifying your funded ratio can help guarantee you're on track for a secure and enjoyable retirement.

Chapter 6:

Managing Retirement Accounts and Withdrawals

Managing retirement savings and withdrawals is a vital component of achieving financial stability and longevity in retirement. Here's a complete guide to assist you in successfully traversing this process:

Understanding retirement accounts

Retirement accounts, such as 401(k), IRAs, and Roth IRAs, are intended to help you save for retirement while providing tax advantages. Managing these accounts entails regular monitoring, adjusting your portfolio, and making strategic contributions and payouts.

- **Withdrawal Strategies:** The 4% Rule advocates taking 4% of your retirement account in the first year and adjusting for inflation annually. It tries to generate a consistent income stream while protecting the investment.

- Withdraw a certain percentage of your portfolio annually. This strategy regulates withdrawals based on portfolio performance, which helps to avoid draining your assets too soon.
- **Fixed Dollar Withdrawals:** Withdraw a fixed amount annually. This generates consistent income but may not adjust for inflation or changes in your financial needs.
- **Bucket Strategy:** Organize your assets into "buckets" based on future financial needs. Short-term buckets contain safer assets for immediate requirements, while long-term buckets may be more actively invested.

The Total Return Approach focuses on the overall return of your portfolio, including interest, dividends, and capital gains. Withdrawals are based on the overall return, allowing for flexibility and future growth.

Required Minimum Distributions (RMDs).
The IRS requires that you begin taking RMDs on regular IRAs and 401(k)s at the age of 73. Failure to take RMDs might lead to severe tax

penalties. Roth IRAs, on the other hand, have no required minimum distributions, allowing your investments to grow tax-free for a longer period of time.

Tax considerations
Managing withdrawals in a tax-efficient manner is critical. Withdrawals from traditional retirement accounts are taxed as ordinary income, whereas Roth IRA withdrawals are often tax-free. Strategically determining which accounts to draw from can help you reduce your tax burden.

Practical Tips
Review your retirement plan annually to account for market fluctuations, health changes, and spending demands.
Diversify withdrawals by withdrawing from both taxable and tax-advantaged accounts to balance tax obligations.

Effective retirement account and withdrawal management ensures that you can continue to live the lifestyle you want without running out of money. You can develop a long-term financial plan for your retirement years by knowing different withdrawal techniques, following RMD laws, and taking tax implications into account.

Traditional IRAs vs. Roth IRAs: Choosing the Best Fit

Let's look at the basic differences between Traditional IRAs and Roth IRAs, and then talk about which one is ideal for different tax situations and retirement goals.

Traditional IRA

- **Tax Treatment:** Traditional IRAs allow for pre-tax contributions, resulting in a tax deduction in the year of contribution.
- **Withdrawals:** When you withdraw money in retirement, it is taxed like ordinary income.
- **Contribution Limits:** In 2024, the annual contribution limit is $6,500 (or $7,500 for individuals over 50).

Required Minimum Distributions (RMDs):
Start receiving Required Minimum Distributions (RMDs) at age 73.

Early withdrawals before age 59½ are subject to a 10% penalty and income tax, with limited exceptions.

Roth IRA contributions are made with post-tax monies and do not result in a tax deduction.

Withdrawals are tax-free in retirement if certain requirements are met. Contribution limits are the same as in Traditional IRAs: $6,500 per year (or $7,500 if 50 or older) for 2024.

There are no required minimum distributions (RMDs) for account holders during their lifetime.

Contributions can be withdrawn at any moment without incurring taxes or charges. If the account is at least five years old and withdrawn beyond age 59½, earnings are tax-free.

Which Account Is Best?

1. Taxation Situations:

- **Traditional IRA:** Useful if you plan to be in a lower tax band in retirement. The instant tax deduction can help you reduce your taxable income right away. Roth IRAs are ideal if you expect to be in a higher tax bracket in retirement. Paying taxes today at a reduced rate may save you money in the long term.

2. Retirement goals:

- **Traditional IRA:** Ideal if you wish to reduce your taxable income now while deferring taxes until retirement.
- **Roth IRA:** Ideal if you desire tax-free income in retirement and want more control over withdrawals.

- **Traditional IRA:** Provides immediate tax benefits and is advantageous if you anticipate a lesser income in retirement.
- **Roth IRA:** Allows for tax-free withdrawals in retirement, which is favorable if you expect to earn more in retirement.

The choice between a Traditional IRA and a Roth IRA is determined by your present tax situation and future aspirations. It is generally beneficial to talk with a financial expert to personalize the selection to your specific needs.

Strategies for Tax-Efficient Withdrawals

When preparing for retirement, it is critical to examine how to withdraw funds in a tax-efficient manner. Here are some ideas for minimizing tax liabilities:

Withdraw from taxable accounts. First, withdraw from taxable accounts (e.g., brokerage accounts) to benefit from lower long-term capital gains tax rates.

This enables tax-deferred accounts (such as Traditional IRAs) to continue to grow tax-free for an extended period.

Consider converting some of your Traditional IRA holdings to Roth IRAs. This is especially useful in years when your income is modest because you will pay taxes on the conversion at a possibly reduced rate.

Once in a Roth IRA, subsequent withdrawals are tax-free if certain conditions are met.

Plan your withdrawals to stay in lower tax brackets. For example, if you are approaching the threshold of a higher tax rate, limit your withdrawals to avoid entering the higher bracket.

Be aware of the Required Minimum Distributions (RMDs) from Traditional IRAs and 401(k)s beginning at age 73.

Qualified Charitable Distributions:

If you are 70½ or older, you can make QCDs from your IRA to a qualified charity. This can satisfy your RMD without raising your taxable income.

The "Bucket" Strategy

The "bucket" concept is a popular way to manage withdrawals throughout retirement. It entails categorizing your retirement resources into distinct "buckets" based on time horizons and risk levels:

- **Bucket 1:** Short-Term Needs (0–5 Years)
  This bucket is for immediate costs and should be filled with low-risk, highly liquid assets such as cash, money market funds, or short-term bonds.
  It ensures that you have adequate funds to cover living expenses and emergencies without having to liquidate investments at a loss.

- **Bucket 2:** Mid-Term Needs (5–10 years)
  This bucket is for mid-term expenses that can be placed in a mix of bonds and dividend-paying companies.

It seeks to strike a balance between growth and stability.

- **Bucket 3:** Long-Term Needs (more than 10 years)
  This bucket is intended for long-term growth and can be invested in riskier assets such as equities and real estate.

The idea is to earn larger returns over time, which can help beat inflation and boost your retirement funds.

Implementing the Bucket Strategy.

Assess your retirement goals and expenses to determine how much to allocate to each category.

For example, you could allocate 2-3 years of living expenditures to Bucket 1, 5-10 years to Bucket 2, and the balance to Bucket.

Rebalance buckets periodically to meet changing needs and market conditions.

Replenish Bucket 1 from Bucket 2 as needed, and Bucket 2 from Bucket.

Adjust for inflation when planning withdrawals to maintain purchasing power over time.

Combining tax-efficient withdrawal options with the bucket approach allows you to properly manage your retirement funds while minimizing taxes and ensuring a consistent income stream throughout your retirement.

Required Minimum Distributions (RMDs) and Penalties to Avoid

Required Minimum Distributions (RMDs) are the minimum sums that must be withdrawn each year from some retirement accounts once you reach a particular age. These accounts include standard IRAs, 401(k)s, SEP IRAs, and SIMPLE IRAs. The goal of RMDs is to ensure that people eventually pay taxes on their retirement savings.

How Does RMD Work?

- **Starting Age:** You must begin taking RMDs on April 1 of the year following your age 73. Afterwards, RMDs must be taken by December 31 of each year.
- **Calculation:** The RMD amount is computed by dividing the account balance as of December 31 of the preceding year by a life expectancy

factor established by the IRS. This component differs depending on your age and, in some situations, the age of your spouse.

- **Multiple Accounts:** If you have multiple IRAs, you must calculate the RMD for each one separately, but you can withdraw the entire amount from one or more. RMDs must be taken from each 401(k) account individually.

- **Penalties:** Failure to take the full RMD carries a significant penalty—25% of the amount not withdrawn.

Strategies for avoiding penalties and minimizing taxes.

- **Calculate accurately:** Calculate the correct RMD amount using the IRS life expectancy tables. Your account custodian can help with this.

- **Take RMDs on time:** Avoid penalties by completing your RMDs by the dates. Consider taking your first RMD by December 31 of the year you turn 73 to avoid having to take two RMDs in the same year.

- **Qualified Charitable Distributions:** If you are 70½ or older, you can transfer up to $100,000 per year from your IRA to an eligible charity. This transfer contributes to your RMD but is not taxable income.

- **Roth IRA conversions:** Convert some of your traditional IRA money to a Roth IRA before hitting the RMD age. RMDs are not necessary for Roth IRAs while the account owner is alive. If you are still working and do not own more than 5% of the company, you can suspend RMDs from your current employer's 401(k) until retirement.
- The Qualified Longevity Annuity Contract (QLAC) Invest in a QLAC, which allows you to defer up to 25% of your retirement account balance (up to $145,000) until the age of 85.

Understanding RMDs and applying these techniques can allow you to better manage your retirement withdrawals, avoid fines, and reduce your tax burden.

Chapter 7:

Healthcare and Long-Term Care Planning

Healthcare and long-term care planning are critical components of future preparedness, ensuring that you and your loved ones receive the care and assistance they require as you age or experience health issues.

Healthcare Planning
Healthcare planning entails making decisions about your medical treatment in advance. This includes:

- **Advance Directives:** Legal documents such as living wills and durable powers of attorney for healthcare allow you to declare your medical preferences and appoint someone to make decisions for you if you become unable to do so.
- **Health Insurance:** Ensuring you have proper health insurance coverage is

critical. This includes learning about your Medicare alternatives, supplemental insurance, and any long-term care insurance coverage.

- **Regular Check-Ups:** Regular medical check-ups and screenings can help discover and control health issues early on, enhancing your quality of life and potentially lowering the need for long-term care.

Long-term Care Planning

Long-term care (LTC) refers to a variety of services designed to address personal and health-care needs over a prolonged period. Planning for long-term care includes:

- **Assessing Needs:** Determine the level of care you may require depending on your health, family history, and lifestyle. This can include home care, assisted living, and nursing facility care.
- **Financial Planning:** Because long-term care can be costly, it is critical to prepare how you will pay for these services. Personal savings, long-term care insurance, and government initiatives like Medicaid are among the available options.

- **Choosing Care Options:** Investigate various forms of care, including home-based care, community services, and residential institutions. Each alternative has advantages and disadvantages, and the ideal pick is based on personal needs and tastes.

Strategies for Effective Planning.
- **Start early:** The greatest time to plan for healthcare and long-term care is before you need it. Early planning enables you to make informed decisions and prevent hasty decisions during a crisis.
- **Involve the family:** Discuss your plans with family members to ensure that they understand and can help you carry them out.
- **Legal and Financial Advice:** Consult with legal and financial professionals to ensure that your plans are complete and legally sound. They can assist with estate planning, trust creation, and insurance selection.
- **Stay informed:** Keep up with changes to healthcare regulations, insurance policies, and long-term care alternatives.

This knowledge will enable you to change your strategies as needed.

By following these actions, you may ensure that you get the care you require while putting less financial burden and worry on your loved ones. Planning ahead of time gives you peace of mind and contributes to your quality of life as you get older.

Planning for Medical Expenses in Retirement

Planning for healthcare bills in retirement is critical to maintaining financial security. Here's a breakdown of the main components and how to prepare for them:

1. Medicare premiums.
- **Medicare Part A (Hospital Insurance):** Most people do not pay a Part A premium if they or their spouse paid Medicare taxes while working. If you do not qualify for premium-free Part A, your monthly premium could be up to $505 in 2024.
- **Medicare Part B (Medical insurance):** The regular monthly Part B premium in 2024 is $174.70. This

premium could be greater depending on your income.

- **Medicare Part D (Prescription Drug Benefits):** Premiums vary by plan and income. In 2024, the average monthly premium will be approximately $32.74.

2. Deductibles

The Part A deductible for each benefit period in 2024 is $1,632.

In 2024, the Part B yearly deductible will be $240.

3. Out-of-pocket expenses.

- **Coinsurance and copayments:** After meeting the Part A deductible, you will pay nothing for the first 60 days of inpatient hospital care. The cost for days 61-90 is $408 per day, while days 91-150 are $816 per day. After achieving the deductible, Part B normally requires you to pay 20% of the Medicare-approved cost for most doctor services, outpatient therapy, and durable medical equipment.
- **Medicare Advantage Plans:** These plans typically have cheaper out-of-pocket expenses but may require

you to use network providers. They also have an out-of-pocket maximum, but original Medicare does not.

4. Planning for Healthcare Costs.

- **Health Savings Accounts (HSA):** If you have a high-deductible health plan before retiring, you can make contributions to an HSA. The funds can be utilized tax-free for eligible medical expenses, such as Medicare premiums. Consider getting long-term care insurance to cover services that are not covered by Medicare, such as extended nursing facility stays.
- **Budgeting:** Determine your annual healthcare costs and incorporate them into your retirement plan. The average retired couple at age 65 may expect to spend approximately $315,000 on healthcare bills during retirement.

5. Additional Tips

Review Your Medicare Options Annually: Medicare plans and your health needs can vary, so it's critical to check your coverage options every year during the open enrollment period.

Consider Supplemental Insurance: Medigap coverage can help with costs that Original Medicare does not cover, such as copayments, coinsurance, and deductibles.

Planning ahead and recognizing these fees will help you better manage your money in retirement.

Medicare and Supplemental Coverage: What You Need to Know

Medicare is a government health insurance program designed largely for those over the age of 65, but it also covers some younger people with impairments. It consists of four major parts:

Hospice care, skilled nursing facility care, inpatient hospital stays, and certain home health services are all covered by Medicare Part A.

Medicare Part A.
- **Cost:** Most people do not have to pay a Part A premium if they or their spouse paid Medicare taxes while working. If

not, the premium may reach $505 per month in 2024.

Medicare Part B (Medical insurance)
Coverage includes outpatient treatment, doctor visits, preventive programs, and some home health care.
- **Cost:** The regular monthly Part B premium in 2024 is $174.70. Your income may determine a greater amount. In addition, there is a $240 annual deductible.

Part C (Medicare Advantage)
Private insurance businesses offer Medicare Part C (Medicare Advantage) coverage as an alternative to Original Medicare Parts A and B. These plans frequently offer extra benefits like vision, dental, and hearing care, as well as prescription drug coverage.
- **Cost varies by plan and provider.** These plans typically have cheaper out-of-pocket expenses but may require you to use network providers.

Medicare Part D
Prescription Drug Coverage
- **Coverage:** Helps with the expense of prescription medications.

Premiums vary depending on plan and income. In 2024, the average monthly premium will be approximately $32.74.

Private firms sell Medigap policies to cover costs not covered by Original Medicare, including copayments, coinsurance, and deductibles.

When Needed: If you have Original Medicare (Parts A and B) and need assistance with out-of-pocket expenses, a Medigap policy may be advantageous. It is especially important if you anticipate numerous medical visits or have chronic diseases that necessitate continuing care.

When to Consider Supplemental Coverage.

- **High out-of-pocket expenses:** If you expect significant out-of-pocket expenses, Medigap can help you manage them.
- **Travel:** If you travel frequently, several Medigap policies include coverage for medical care outside the United States.
- **Comprehensive Coverage:** If you want more comprehensive coverage than what Original Medicare provides, Medigap can fill the gaps.

Understanding these components, as well as the significance of supplemental coverage, will allow you to make more informed healthcare decisions in retirement.

Long-Term Care Insurance: Is It Right for You?

Long-term care insurance is intended to cover services that help with daily living activities such as bathing, dressing, and eating but are not normally covered by conventional health insurance or Medicare. This sort of insurance may cover care provided in a variety of settings, such as your home, a nursing home, an assisted living facility, or an adult daycare center.

Who Should Get Long-Term Care Insurance?
Long-term care insurance is especially useful for those who:

- **Have a Family History of Chronic Illnesses:** If your family history includes Alzheimer's disease or other chronic illnesses, you may be more likely to require long-term care.
  Want to protect savings and assets?
  Long-term care can be extremely

expensive, and insurance can help protect your savings and assets from being exhausted by these expenses.

- **Prefer More Care Options:** If you have insurance, you may be able to choose between different care settings and professionals.
- **Are Between the Ages 50-65:** Premiums are typically lower if you buy insurance when you are young and healthy.

Checklist for determining if long-term care insurance is necessary.

Here's a checklist to help you decide whether long-term care insurance is best for you.

Health considerations

- *Do you have a family history of chronic diseases or ailments that necessitate extended care?*
- *Are you in good health now, making it easier to qualify for coverage with a lower premium?*

Family History

- *Have your parents or close relatives required long-term care services?*

- *Is there a history of longevity in your family that increases the likelihood of requiring long-term care?*

Financial and budgetary considerations
- *Can you afford the premiums while maintaining your existing lifestyle and retirement savings?*
- *Do you have considerable assets that you wish to safeguard from the high costs of long-term care?*
- *Have you considered the future costs of long-term care and how they may affect your financial situation?*

Personal Preferences
- *Do you like greater control over your care options and settings?*
- *Are you concerned about being a financial burden for your family?*

Additional Tips:
Research and compare policies: Examine various policies and providers to locate one that meets your needs and budget.
- **Consider Inflation Protection:** This might assist in ensuring that your benefits keep up with the escalating cost of healthcare.

- **Consult a Financial Advisor:** They can explain how long-term care insurance fits into your overall retirement strategy.

Long-term care insurance can provide financial security and peace of mind, but you should carefully analyze your individual circumstances before making a decision.

Chapter 8:

Self-Managing Your Retirement vs. Hiring a Professional

Retirement planning is an important process that must be done carefully, taking into account your financial goals, risk tolerance, and investing techniques. Whether to self-manage your retirement or employ a professional is a big decision.

Here's a full comparison to help you decide which technique is right for you.

Pros of Self-Managed Retirement:

Cost Savings: By managing your own retirement, you avoid paying fees to financial counselors or planners, which can result in significant savings over time.
Control: You have complete control over your financial decisions and tactics. This may be especially appealing if you have a thorough

understanding of financial markets and investment fundamentals.

Flexibility: You can update your portfolio at any moment without consulting a professional, allowing for quick modifications in response to market conditions or personal circumstances.

Cons:

- **Time-consuming:** Managing your own retirement demands a significant time commitment to research, monitor, and change your investments.
- **Knowledge and expertise:** Without a thorough understanding of financial planning and investment techniques, you could make decisions that jeopardize your retirement resources.
- **Emotional Decision-Making:** It can be difficult to remain impartial about your investments, particularly amid market turbulence. Emotional decisions might result in poor investment choices.

Pros:

- **Expertise and Experience:** Financial counselors and planners bring extensive expertise and experience to the table.

They can offer specialized advice based on your unique financial circumstances and objectives.

- **Comprehensive preparation:** Professionals may assist with all elements of retirement preparation, including tax strategies, estate planning, and risk mitigation.
- **Peace of Mind:** Knowing that your retirement is being managed by a professional can help to alleviate stress and give you confidence that your financial future is secure.

Cons:

- **Cost:** Hiring a professional might be costly. Advisors often charge fees based on a proportion of the assets under management, hourly rates, or fixed fees.
- **Less influence:** You may have less direct influence over your investments because advisors frequently make decisions based on their knowledge and the approach you agreed on.
- **Finding the Right Counsel:** It might be difficult to locate a reliable and qualified counsel who shares your financial objectives and principles.

The decision to self-manage your retirement or hire a professional is based on your financial expertise, time availability, and level of comfort with managing investments. If you have the knowledge and time, self-management can be both cost-effective and empowering. However, if you prefer experienced advice and a complete approach, hiring a professional may be the best option. Consider your specific circumstances and long-term goals while making retirement planning decisions.

The Pros and Cons of Managing Your Own Portfolio

The advantages and disadvantages of self-managing retirement portfolios include:

- **Control and Flexibility:** You have complete control over your investing decisions, allowing you to personalize your portfolio to meet your unique objectives and risk tolerance.
- **Cost Savings:** Managing your own portfolio allows you to save on advisor fees and other management costs.
  Managing your own investments can enhance your understanding of financial

markets. Additionally, you can customize your investment options to include non-traditional assets such as real estate.

Drawbacks:

Time-consuming: Successful portfolio management needs extensive research and monitoring.

Mistake Risk: Without professional help, you are more likely to make investment mistakes that will have an impact on your retirement savings.

Portfolio management requires an understanding of complicated financial instruments and market dynamics.

Emotional judgments: Personal biases and emotional responses to market swings might result in poor financial judgments.

- **Tools and Resources for DIY Retirement Management Betterment App:** Create a retirement plan, track spending, and alter investments as needed.
- **The Charles Schwab Retirement Calculator** is a free tool that estimates

if your funds will cover your retirement expenditures.

- **The Retirement Inspired Quotient (R:IQ) Tool:** Estimates how much you can anticipate having in retirement based on your existing investments.
- **Fidelity Retirement Score:** Provides a full assessment of your retirement preparation and recommends changes.
- Empower Retirement Planner is a sophisticated tool for mapping out your retirement funds and investments.
- The Stash Retirement Calculator can help you plan your retirement savings and investment strategy.
- The NewRetirement Calculator provides a complete analysis of your retirement plan, including income, expenses, and savings.

These tools can assist you in properly managing your retirement portfolio, giving insights and recommendations to ensure you stay on pace to accomplish your retirement objectives.

How to Choose a Financial Advisor

Choosing a financial advisor is a critical decision for your financial stability. Here are some suggestions and important credentials to consider:

Tips for Selecting a Financial Advisor
- **Identify your needs:** Determine the type of financial guidance you require. Are you interested in retirement planning, investment guidance, tax preparation, or overall financial planning?
- **Check credentials:** Look for consultants with recognized qualifications, such as:
- **Certified Financial Planner (CFP):** This designation indicates a high level of skill in financial planning.
- **Chartered Financial Analyst (CFA):** Focuses on managing investments.
- **Certified Public Accountant (CPA):** A valuable resource for tax planning and accounting.

- **Personal Financial Specialist (PFS):** A CPA with added financial planning experience.
- **Verify their background:** Check the advisor's background and any disciplinary proceedings using sites such as FINRA BrokerCheck or the Securities and Exchange Commission's Investment Adviser Public Disclosure (IAPD).
- **Understand Their Fee Structure:** Advisors may be fee-only, commission-based, or a combination of the two. Fee-only advisors are typically thought to have fewer conflicts of interest.
- **Inquire About Their Approach:** Inquire about their investment philosophy and how they intend to help you accomplish your financial objectives. Make certain that their strategy matches your risk tolerance and financial goals.
- **Get references:** Request references from current or previous clients to gain an understanding of their experience and satisfaction with the advisor's services.
- **Evaluate communication:** Ensure that the advisor communicates properly

and regularly. You should feel free to ask questions and discuss your financial issues.

- **Consider their experience:** Look for advisors that have worked with people in comparable financial conditions to yours.

Questions to Ask Potential Financial Advisors

- What are your qualifications and credentials?
- How much do you charge for your services, and what is your price structure?
- Is it possible for you to provide testimonials from present or former clients?
- What's your investment philosophy?
- How will you assist me attain my financial objectives?
- How frequently will we meet to review my financial plan?
- In addition to investment advice, what other services do you offer?

By carefully evaluating these characteristics and asking the correct questions, you can select a financial advisor who can help you reach your financial objectives.

The Role of Fiduciary Duty in Retirement Planning

Fiduciary duty is a legal and ethical commitment that requires an individual to act in the best interests of another party. In the context of financial advice, a fiduciary is legally required to prioritize their client's interests before their own.

This obligation includes several crucial responsibilities:

- **Duty of Loyalty:** The advisor must act only in the client's best interests while avoiding conflicts of interest.
- **Duty of Care:** The advisor must make decisions with the same care, skill, and diligence as a prudent person.
- **Duty of Good Faith:** The advisor must operate truthfully and in good faith, ensuring that all activities are legal.
- **Duty of Confidentiality:** The adviser must keep the client's information secret and not utilize it for personal benefit.

- **Duty of Disclosure:** The adviser must fully disclose any potential conflicts of interest and all relevant facts that may influence the client's decision.

Importance of Fiduciary Duty in Selecting an Advisor

Choosing an advisor with a fiduciary duty is critical because it assures that the advisor is legally bound to work in your best interests. This can bring peace of mind and trust by ensuring that the advisor's recommendations are made with your financial well-being in mind. Non-fiduciary advisors may be motivated by commissions or other incentives that are not in your best interest.

How Fiduciary Duty Impacts Retirement Outcomes

- **Better Investment Decisions:** Fiduciary advisors are expected to recommend investments that are most appropriate for your financial goals and risk tolerance, which can result in better long-term outcomes.
- **Lower Costs:** Fiduciary advisors must examine the cost-effectiveness of their

advice, potentially saving you money in fees and expenses.

- **Conflict-free Advice:** With a fiduciary, you are less likely to receive advice skewed by the advisor's personal gain, resulting in more impartial and helpful financial planning.
- **Enhanced Trust and Confidence:** Knowing that your adviser is legally required to operate in your best interests can boost your trust in their advice, resulting in a more collaborative and productive planning process.

Choosing a fiduciary advisor ensures that your retirement planning is handled with the utmost care and integrity, resulting in more secure and successful retirement results.

Chapter 9:

Estate Planning and Legacy Building

Estate planning is the act of structuring and managing your assets so that they are dispersed according to your intentions after you die. It entails drafting legal documents such as wills, trusts, and powers of attorney that define how your estate should be managed. The major goals of estate planning are to reduce taxes, avoid probate, and guarantee that your assets are dispersed efficiently and in accordance with your wishes.

Key Elements of Estate Planning:

- **Will:** A legal document stating how your possessions should be dispersed and who will care for any young children.
- **Trusts:** Arrangements in which a third person, or trustee, holds assets on behalf of beneficiaries. Trusts can help you

avoid probate and have more control over asset distribution.

- A power of attorney is a document that designates someone to make financial or medical decisions for you if you become incapacitated.
- **Beneficiary designations:** Designating beneficiaries for retirement accounts, life insurance policies, and other financial accounts to ensure that they be passed directly to the designated receivers.
- **Healthcare Directives:** Instructions for medical care if you are unable to communicate your preferences.

Legacy Building extends beyond the financial issues of estate planning. It entails leaving a lasting legacy by transferring not only assets but also values, beliefs, and traditions to future generations. Legacy planning focuses on the bigger picture of what you want to leave behind, such as charitable contributions, family values, and personal tales.

Key Components of Legacy Building:

- **Charitable Giving:** Creating foundations or donating to causes that match your principles and interests.
- **Family Values and customs:** Documenting and passing down family history, customs, and values to ensure their survival for future generations.
- **Education Funds:** Creating funds to support the education of children or grandchildren, providing they have the necessary means to succeed.
- **Personal letters and ethical wills:** Write letters or ethical wills to communicate your life lessons, values, and future goals with your loved ones.

Importance of Estate Planning and Legacy Development:

- **Financial Security:** Ensures that your loved ones are financially secure, and that your assets are handled and distributed in accordance with your instructions.
- **Minimizing Conflicts:** By explicitly articulating your intentions, you can reduce the likelihood of heir disputes.

- **Tax Efficiency:** Reduces estate taxes and other expenses, leaving more of your fortune for your beneficiaries.
- **Personal Fulfillment:** Provides a sense of fulfillment knowing that your legacy will favorably effect future generations while reflecting your values and beliefs.

By combining estate planning and legacy building, you can develop a comprehensive strategy that not only protects your financial assets but also guarantees that your beliefs and traditions are carried forward, creating a meaningful and long-lasting impact on your family and community.

Creating a Will and Trust: Essential Documents

Having a will and trust in place is important for various reasons:

Significance of a Will and Trust
Control Over Asset Distribution: With a will, you can specify how your assets should be transferred after your death, ensuring that your intentions are fulfilled. Without a will, state laws will dictate distribution, which may differ from your preferences.

Trusts can help you avoid the time-consuming and expensive probate process. This implies that your beneficiaries will be able to access your assets faster and with fewer legal impediments.

Protecting young Children: With a will, you can name guardians for your young children, ensuring they are cared for by someone you trust.

Privacy: Unlike wills, which become public records during probate, trusts can stay secret, keeping your financial information private.

Tax Advantages: Trusts can reduce estate taxes and shield assets from creditors.

Step-by-Step Guide to Making a Will.

- **List your assets:** Identify all of your assets, including property, investments, and personal items.

- **Select Beneficiaries:** Find out your assets' inheritable successors.

- **Select an executor:** Appoint someone you can trust to carry out the terms of your will.

- **Name the guardians for minor children:** If you have children, assign guardians for them.

- **Draft the Will:** You can utilize online templates or hire an attorney to create your will.
- **Sign the will:** As needed by state law, sign your will under the observation of witnesses.
- **Store the Will Safely:** Keep your will in a secure place and notify your executor of its position.
- **Review and Update:** You should review and update your will on a regular basis to reflect changes in your life.

Step-by-Step Guide to Establishing Trust

- **Determine the purpose:** Determine the reason why you need a trust.
- **Select the Type of Trust:** Choose the form of trust that best meets your needs (revocable, irrevocable, or special needs).
- **Identify the trustee and beneficiaries:** Choose a trustee to oversee the trust and beneficiaries to receive the assets.
- **Transfer Assets:** Move your assets to the trust. This may entail changing titles and deeds.
- **Draft the Trust Document:** Collaborate with an attorney to draft the

trust document, including the terms and conditions.

- **Sign the trust document:** Put your signature on the document while a notary public watches.
- **Fund the Trust:** Ensure that all planned assets have been moved to the trust.
- **Review and Update:** Make sure the trust still represents your actual intentions and situation by reviewing and updating it from time to time.

Creating a will and trust can bring peace of mind by ensuring that your possessions and loved ones are cared for accordance to your preferences.

Planning for Your Beneficiaries and Legacy

Choosing beneficiaries and deciding how to leave a legacy need careful consideration of your values, relationships, and long-term objectives. Here's a guide to help you make these critical decisions:

Making decisions about beneficiaries.

- **Identify your priorities:** Think about your most significant values. This could be family, friends, philanthropic organizations, or institutions that have made a big difference in your life.
- **Assess needs and relationships:** Consider the financial requirements and conditions of possible beneficiaries. Consider who depends on you financially and who would gain the most from your assets.
- **Communicate your intentions:** Discuss your plans with possible beneficiaries to ensure they understand your intentions and prevent future conflicts.
- **Consider equal vs. unequal distribution:** Determine whether you want to distribute your assets equally among beneficiaries or whether there are valid reasons for asymmetrical distribution (for example, one child has larger financial requirements).
- **Update regularly:** Life circumstances change, so be sure your beneficiary designations reflect your current relationships and interests.

Strategies for Passing Wealth

- **Direct Gifts:** In your will or trust, you can designate specific assets or sums of money for your beneficiaries.
- **Trusts:** Setting up trusts can provide your beneficiaries more flexibility over how and when they receive their inheritance. Trusts can also provide tax advantages and shield assets from creditors.
- **Consider giving a portion of your estate to a charitable organization:** This can be accomplished by direct donations, charity trusts, or donor-advised funds.
- Set up education accounts or 529 plans for your children or grandchildren to cover their future educational expenses.
- **Life Insurance:** Designate beneficiaries for your life insurance plans so that they can get financial support after your death.
- **Retirement Accounts:** Designate beneficiaries for your retirement accounts (e.g., 401(k), IRA) to ensure that the assets are handed directly to them without going through probate.
- **Family Business Succession:** If you own a family business, develop a succession plan to ensure a smooth

handover and the business's long-term prosperity.

Leave a legacy.

- **Create a Legacy Letter:** Write a letter to your loved ones that expresses your ideals, life lessons, and future goals. This might be a significant method to share your knowledge and affection.
- **Philanthropy:** Create a foundation or endowment in your name to provide long-term support for issues you care about.
- **Memorial Funds:** Create a memorial fund to benefit a certain cause or organization in your honor.
- **Personal artifacts:** Pass along family heirlooms, photos, and other sentimental artifacts.
- **Community Involvement:** Encourage your family to carry on your tradition of community service and involvement.

By carefully arranging your inheritance and taking into account your beneficiaries' needs and values, you can leave a legacy that reflects your life and priorities.

Minimizing Estate Taxes and Probate Costs

Tips for minimizing estate taxes

Gifting Assets: You can lower the size of your taxable estate by transferring assets to your beneficiaries during your lifetime. The yearly gift tax exception permits you to give up to $17,000 per person each year without paying gift taxes.

Charitable Donations: Donating to charities might lower your taxable estate. Charitable remainder trusts (CRTs) and charitable lead trusts (CLTs) are useful tools in this situation.

Irrevocable Life Insurance Trusts (ILITs): Placing a life insurance policy in an ILIT exempts the death benefit from your taxable estate.

Family Limited Partnerships (FLPs): These allow family members to transfer business interests at a lower tax rate while maintaining control over the business.

Grantor Retained Annuity Trusts (GRATs): GRATs enable you to transfer appreciating assets to beneficiaries while minimizing gift tax consequences.

Tips for avoiding probate.

- **Revocable Living Trust:** A revocable living trust transfers assets directly to beneficiaries after death, avoiding probate. Joint ownership with rights of survivorship assures property passes directly to co-owners without probate.

- **Payment-on-Death (POD) and Transfer-on-Death (TOD) Accounts:** To avoid probate, you might designate beneficiaries for bank and financial accounts. Ensure that all of your retirement accounts, life insurance policies, and other financial accounts have current beneficiary designations.

In some states, tiny estates may be eligible for simplified probate proceedings, which are specdier and less expensive.

Example of Trusts and Other Estate Planning Tools
- **Revocable Trusts:** These trusts can be changed or revoked by the grantor throughout their lifetime. They add flexibility and help to avoid probate.
- **Irrevocable Trusts:** Once established, these trusts cannot be modified without the beneficiary's permission. They offer

asset protection as well as major tax advantages.

- **Special Needs Trusts:** Designed to provide for a disabled recipient while maintaining their eligibility for government benefits.
- **Charitable Trusts:** These include charitable remainder trusts (CRTs) and charitable lead trusts (CLTs), which provide income for beneficiaries while also benefiting a charity.
- **Bypass Trusts:** Also known as credit shelter trusts, these allow married couples to fully benefit from estate tax exemptions.
- **Qualified Personal Residence Trusts (QPRTs):** These allow you to pass your house to beneficiaries at a lower gift tax value while keeping the right to live in it for a set term.
- **Generation-Skipping Trusts:** These trusts enable you to transfer assets to grandkids while skipping the children and potentially lowering estate taxes.

Using these tactics and resources, you may successfully manage your estate, reduce taxes, and guarantee that your assets are transferred how you choose.

Chapter 10:

Common Retirement Pitfalls and How to Avoid Them

Planning for retirement is critical, yet many people make typical mistakes that risk their financial stability. Here are some of the most common mistakes and ways to avoid them:

1. Failure to Start Early Enough: Procrastinating retirement savings can dramatically reduce your accumulation owing to compound interest.

- **Solution:** Begin saving as early as possible. Even tiny contributions might accumulate significantly over time. To optimize your investments, consider employer-sponsored retirement plans and individual retirement accounts (IRAs).

2. Underestimating Retirement Expenses: Many retirees underestimate the amount needed to maintain their lifestyle, resulting in financial shortages.

- **Solution:** Create a detailed retirement budget that accounts for all prospective expenses, such as healthcare, housing, and recreational activities. Consider talking with a financial professional to ensure your predictions are accurate.

3. Relying solely on Social Security: This can result in insufficient income, as these payments only cover a percentage of your pre-retirement wages.

- **Solution:** Diversify your retirement income streams. This can include savings, investments, pensions, and part-time work. Make sure you have a thorough strategy that isn't just based on Social Security.

4. Ignoring Inflation: Failure to account for inflation can lead to decreased buying power and difficulty covering expenses.

- **Solution:** Invest in assets that can outperform inflation, such as equities and real estate. To keep up with inflation, assess your investing strategy on a regular basis and make adjustments.

5. Poor investment choices.
- **Pitfall:** Making too conservative or risky investing decisions can limit your growth potential or expose you to substantial losses.

- **Solution:** Create a balanced investment portfolio that matches your risk tolerance and time horizon. Diversify your investments to spread the risk, and seek professional guidance if necessary.

6. Lack of a Withdrawal Strategy: Failure to plan withdrawals can lead to premature depletion of resources and missed tax benefits.

- **Solution:** Develop a withdrawal strategy that accounts for tax consequences and ensures your funds last until your retirement. This could include withdrawing from taxable accounts first and then from tax-advantaged ones.

7. Underestimating healthcare expenses: This can cause financial difficulty, especially as costs rise.

- **Solution:** Plan for healthcare bills by looking into long-term care insurance and setting aside money expressly for medical expenses. Understand your Medicare options and any supplemental coverage you may require.

8. Failing to update your plan.
- **Pitfall:** Life changes such as marriage, divorce, or childbirth can all have an influence on your retirement strategy. Failure to update your plan can cause gaps in your financial stability.

- **Solution:** Review and adjust your retirement plan on a regular basis to account for changes in your life and finances. Stay up to date on changes to tax laws and retirement benefits that may affect your plan.

Knowing these frequent traps and taking proactive efforts to prevent them will help you protect your financial future and enjoy a pleasant retirement.

Overestimating Your Financial Resources

Common Ways Retirees overestimate their resources.

Underestimating Longevity: Many retirees fail to plan for the prospect of living longer than planned, which might result in them outliving their funds.

Overlooking Healthcare expenses: Retirees frequently underestimate the rising expenses of healthcare, particularly long-term care, which can have a substantial impact on their finances.

Assume Consistent Investment Returns: Expecting consistent, high returns on investments without accounting for market instability might lead to an overestimation of available resources.

Ignoring Inflation: Failure to account for inflation's impact on purchasing power might lead to an overestimation of the true value of retirement savings.

Overestimate Social Security Benefits: Relying too much on Social Security without comprehending the true benefits can result in a gap in expected income.

Neglecting Taxes: Failure to account for taxes on retirement income, such as withdrawals from traditional IRAs and 401(k)s, can lower the amount available.

Strategies for realistic financial assessments.

- **Create a detailed budget:** Create a thorough budget that accounts for all prospective expenses, such as housing, healthcare, travel, and leisure activities. Be realistic about your spending patterns and change as necessary.

- **Plan For Longevity:** Use conservative life expectancy calculations to ensure that your savings last. Consider planning for at least 20 to 30 years of retirement.

- **Consider Healthcare Costs:** Include expected healthcare costs in your budget. Think about long-term care insurance and make medical expense savings plans.

- **Adjust for inflation:** Estimate future expenses and income using inflation-adjusted statistics. This helps to preserve the purchasing power of your funds over time.

- **Diversify income sources:** Do not rely only on Social Security. Diversify your income by including pensions, savings, investments, and part-time work, if possible.
- **Understand the Tax Implications:** Be aware of the tax implications for your retirement income. Consult a financial advisor to design tax-efficient exit plans.
- **Regularly Review and Adjust:** Your financial plan should be reviewed and adjusted on a regular basis to reflect changes in your personal circumstances, market conditions, and financial goals.

Taking these steps will allow you to develop a more accurate and realistic financial plan for retirement, ensuring that your resources last throughout your retirement years.

Not Accounting for Changing Needs in Retirement

Retirement demands alter over time owing to a variety of circumstances, including changes in health, lifestyle, inflation, and unforeseen life events. Here's how these demands fluctuate and how to update your retirement plans on a frequent basis:

Retirement Needs' Impact on Health and Longevity

Early retirement typically means greater health and reduced expenses.

Mid-retirement: Health difficulties may occur, raising medical costs.

Late retirement: High healthcare costs and possibly long-term care needs.

Lifestyle changes may include more travel and leisure activities during early childhood.

Settling Down: In later years, travel may decrease while home-related expenses increase.

Inflation affects daily expenses and healthcare bills.

Unexpected life events, such as the loss of a spouse, market downturns, or family emergencies, can have an impact on financial security.

Guide for Updating Retirement Plans Regularly

- **Annual Review:** To ensure a successful retirement, gather financial documents, review goals, analyze investments, adjust allocations, check savings, evaluate insurance coverage, and update estate planning documents. Regularly review your retirement goals, investments, savings, insurance coverage, and will to ensure financial stability.

- **Assess Financial Goals:** Revisit retirement plans and adjust for changes in lifestyle or priorities.
- Update your budget by tracking your spending and making adjustments to reflect current expenses and future estimates.
- Check for enough health and long-term care insurance coverage.
- **Preventive treatment:** Keep up with health screenings and preventive treatment to save money and improve your health.

Investment strategy:

Risk Tolerance: Base your investing portfolio on your age and risk tolerance. Typically, risk decreases as you age.

Diversification: Diversify your investments to reduce risk.

Accommodate for Inflation: To accommodate for inflation, adjust your withdrawal rate based on the cost of living. The

4% rule is a popular guideline; however, it may need to be tweaked depending on inflation.

Estate Planning: Update documents. Keep your will, powers of attorney, and trusts up to date on a regular basis.

Beneficiaries: Check that beneficiary designations on accounts and insurance policies are current.

Social Security and Pensions: Optimal Timing. Determine the ideal timing to begin receiving Social Security benefits to optimize your earnings.

Pension Options: Consider your pension plan options and select the one that best meets your requirements.

Emergency fund: Savings. Maintain an emergency fund to cover unforeseen needs without jeopardizing your retirement plans.

Regularly assessing and revising your retirement plan allows you to better react to changes and provide a more secure and happier retirement.

Avoiding the "Retirement Gimmick" Trap

Retirement "gimmicks" and scams include high-yield investment schemes that promise huge returns with minimal risk. These are frequently Ponzi schemes in which returns are paid using new investors' funds rather than profit.

- Free Lunch Seminars use high-pressure sales tactics to promote unsuitable or overpriced financial solutions.

- Unregistered investments are dangerous and potentially fraudulent, as they are not registered with regulatory authorities.

- Phishing scams involve emails or phone calls claiming to be from genuine financial institutions in order to collect personal information.

- Annuity scams use misleading information and high-fee products that benefit the seller over the buyer.

- Pyramid schemes include recruiting others to earn money, rather than providing a legal product or service.

- Scammers pose as philanthropic groups to seek donations, often from seniors.

Checklist to Evaluate Financial Products and Services

Verify legitimacy:
- **Regulatory registration:** Ensure that the product or service is registered with the appropriate regulatory organizations (e.g., SEC, FINRA).
- **Company Reputation:** Examine the company's history and reputation using reviews and ratings.

Understand the product:
- **Product Details:** Ensure that you fully grasp how the product works, including its terms and conditions.
- **Risks and Returns:** Evaluate potential risks and achievable returns.

Fees and charges:
- **Transparency:** Ensure that all fees and charges are properly stated.
- **Comparison:** Check fees against similar items to ensure they are reasonable.

Advisor credentials:

- **Qualifications:** Verify the financial advisor's credentials and experience.
- **Fiduciary Duty:** Choose counsel with a fiduciary duty to operate in your best interests.

Performance History:
- **Track Record:** Consider the product or service's past performance.
- **Market Comparison:** Evaluate performance against market benchmarks.

Consult with professionals regarding legal and tax implications. Seek legal and tax guidance to better understand the implications.

Exit Strategy:
- **Liquidity:** Determine how readily you can exit the investment.
- **Penalties:** Be careful of any penalties for premature withdrawal or exit.

- **Red Flags:** Too good to be true. Be skeptical of promises of high rewards at low risk.
- Avoid products sold with high-pressure techniques or tight timeframes.

Documentation:

- **Written Information:** Obtain all information in writing and carefully review it.
- **Contracts:** Before signing any deal, read and understand it thoroughly.

- Consider seeking a second view from an independent financial expert.

Following this checklist can help you protect yourself from scammers and make more informed decisions about financial products and services.

Chapter 11:

The Final Retirement Checkup

A last retirement checkup is a thorough evaluation of your retirement plan to ensure that everything is in order before you retire or as you enter retirement. Here's how to perform a thorough final retirement checkup:

The Final Retirement Checkup

Financial Health Assessment:
- **Saving and Investing:** Evaluate your retirement, savings, and investment portfolios. Ensure that they are in line with your retirement plans.
- **Income Sources:** Confirm all sources of retirement income, such as Social Security, pensions, annuities, and part-time work.

Budget and Expense:

- **Current Budget:** Create a detailed budget that includes all of your retirement expenses.
- **Inflation Adjustment:** Consider inflation to ensure your budget remains realistic over time.

- **Debt Management:** Review outstanding debts and develop a plan to pay them off or manage them efficiently.
- **Mortgage:** Consider paying off your mortgage before retiring.

- **Healthcare Planning:** Review your health insurance coverage, including Medicare and any additional plans.
- **Long-Term Care:** Consider your long-term care insurance alternatives and needs.

- Estate planning involves updating legal documents such as wills, powers of attorney, and healthcare directives.
- **Beneficiaries:** Review and update beneficiary designations for all accounts and insurance.

Lifestyle considerations:

- **Housing:** Decide whether you'll stay in your existing home, downsize, or relocate.
- Plan for hobbies, travel, and other activities to keep you involved and fulfilled.

- Maintain an emergency fund to handle unforeseen needs and avoid interrupting your retirement plan.

- **Tax Planning & Strategy:** Create a tax strategy to reduce taxes on your retirement income.

Required Minimum Distributions (RMDs) To avoid penalties, plan for required minimum distributions from retirement funds.

Professional advice:
- **Financial Advisor:** Work with a financial advisor to assess your retirement plan and make any required changes.
- **Lawyers and tax professionals:** Consult with legal and tax professionals to verify that all components of your plan are addressed.

Regular reviews:

- **Annual Checkup:** Schedule annual assessments of your retirement plan and make any necessary adjustments.

By performing a last retirement checkup, you may retire with confidence, knowing that you have a complete strategy in place to support your financial and personal objectives.

Reviewing Your Plan: Are You Ready to Retire?

Final checklist for determining retirement readiness.

Financial stability:
- **Debt-Free:** Ensure that all debts, including the mortgage, have been paid off or are manageable.
- Maintain an adequate emergency fund to handle any unforeseen expenses.
- **Income Sources:** Confirm all sources of retirement income (such as Social Security, pensions, and annuities).

Budget and Expense:
- Create a detailed budget that covers all planned expenses.

- **Inflation Adjustment:** Consider inflation to ensure your budget remains realistic over time.

- **Healthcare Planning:** Review your health insurance coverage, including Medicare and any additional plans.
- **Long-Term Care:** Consider your long-term care insurance alternatives and needs.

- Estate planning involves updating legal documents such as wills, powers of attorney, and healthcare directives.
- **Beneficiaries:** Review and update beneficiary designations for all accounts and insurance.

Lifestyle considerations:
- **Housing:** Decide whether you'll stay in your existing home, downsize, or relocate.
- Plan for hobbies, travel, and other activities to keep you involved and fulfilled.

- **Tax Planning & Strategy:** Create a tax strategy to reduce taxes on your retirement income.

Required Minimum Distributions (RMDs) To avoid penalties, plan for required minimum distributions from retirement funds.

Investment strategy:
- **Portfolio Review:** Ensure that your investment portfolio is in line with your risk tolerance and retirement objectives.
- **Diversification:** Maintain a diverse portfolio to reduce risk.

Making the final decision.

Evaluate your readiness:
- **Self-Assessment:** Consider your financial, emotional, and physical preparation for retirement.
- **Trial Run:** Consider taking a trial retirement period to evaluate how you adapt to the new lifestyle.

Discuss with family:
- **Family Meeting:** Have open discussions with your family about your retirement intentions and any potential implications for them.

Consider timing:

- **Optimal Timing:** Determine the optimal timing to retire depending on your financial circumstances, health, and personal objectives.
- **Flexibility:** Be prepared to change your retirement date if needed.

Plan for the transition.
- **Gradual Transition:** If possible, ease into retirement by lowering work hours or taking on part-time jobs.
- **Stay Engaged:** Plan activities and interests to keep you busy and engaged in retirement.

Seek professional guidance:
- **Second Opinion:** Seek a second opinion from a financial professional to ensure your plan is sound.
- **Continuous Review:** Review your retirement plan on a regular basis and make any necessary adjustments.

By using this checklist and carefully considering your readiness, you will be able to make an informed decision about when to retire and how to seamlessly transition into this new era of life.

Checklist: 10 Steps Before You Make the Decision

Ten Essential Steps to Take Before Retirement

Assess your financial situation:

- **Action:** Evaluate your funds, investments, and other assets.
- If you haven't already, start recording your expenses and income to have a better understanding of your financial situation.

Create a retirement budget.

- **Action:** Determine your retirement expenses, which include daily living expenses, healthcare, and recreational activities.
- If not finished, start by listing your current spending and adjusting for retirement lifestyle adjustments. To get estimates, use online retirement calculators.

- Aim to become debt-free by paying off mortgages, credit cards, and loans.
- If not completed, create a debt repayment plan that prioritizes high-interest debt first.

Maximize retirement contributions:

- **Action:** Make the maximum contribution to retirement accounts such as 401(k), IRAs, and other savings programs.
- **If Not Completed:** Gradually increase your contributions and take advantage of workplace matches, if available.

To plan for healthcare costs, first understand your needs and insurance options, including Medicare.
If not completed, look into Medicare programs and consider extra insurance. Save for out-of-pocket medical costs.

Determine the Social Security Strategy:

- **Action:** Determine the optimal timing to begin receiving Social Security payments to optimize your income.
- **If Not Completed:** Use Social Security calculators to estimate benefits, and consider deferring them to increase payouts.

- Review and update your estate planning documents, including wills, powers of attorney, and healthcare directives.

- **If Not Completed:** Consult an estate planning attorney to prepare or update these documents.

Evaluate housing options:
- **Action:** Determine if you want to stay in your existing home, downsize, or relocate.
- **If Not Completed:** Determine your housing needs and preferences. Consider the financial and emotional implications of relocation.

- Create an emergency fund to meet unforeseen needs without jeopardizing your retirement savings.
- **If Not Complete:** Begin saving a percentage of your salary on a monthly basis until you have at least 3-6 months' worth of expenses.

Plan for lifestyle changes.
Consider how you plan to spend your retirement years, including hobbies, travel, and social events.
If not finished, begin researching interests and activities that you enjoy. Join a club or group to keep socially active.

Guidelines for Completing These Steps

- **Start Early:** The earlier you start preparing, the more time you'll have to fill any gaps.
- Set realistic goals. Break each stage down into manageable tasks and provide deadlines.
- **Seek Professional Assistance:** Financial experts, estate planners, and healthcare specialists can offer useful advice.
- **Stay Flexible:** Be ready to adapt your plans when circumstances change.
- **Educate yourself:** Continue to learn about retirement planning via books, seminars, and internet resources.

By following these procedures and resolving any gaps, you can assure an easier transition to retirement and a more secure financial future.

Adjusting Your Plan: What to Do If You're Not Ready

If you are not quite ready to retire, there are various tactics you can use to modify your retirement plan. Here are a few key approaches:

1. Delaying retirement

- **Continue Working:** By continuing in the job for a longer period of time, you can continue to make money, which is beneficial in a variety of ways. This allows for increased savings, delayed retirement, and a potential rise in Social Security payments.
- **Delay Social Security Benefits:** If you wait until after your full retirement age to begin receiving benefits, your benefits will increase by around 8% per year until you reach the age of 70. This can dramatically increase your retirement income.

2. Rebalancing portfolios

- **Adjust Asset Allocation:** As you approach retirement, you should examine your investment portfolio. Consider changing to a more conservative asset allocation to reduce risk. This could imply boosting your holdings of bonds and other fixed-income products while minimizing your exposure to equities.
- **Diversify your investments:** Ensure that your portfolio is well-diversified to disperse risk. This may contain a

combination of domestic and international equities, bonds, real estate, and other asset classes.

- **Review and adjust regularly:** Review your portfolio on a regular basis to ensure that it is in line with your risk tolerance and retirement plans. Market conditions and personal situations can vary; therefore, it's critical to alter your plan accordingly.

Additional Considerations:

- **Lessen Debt:** Paying off high-interest debt will help you save more money and lessen financial stress in retirement.
- **Increase Savings:** If possible, contribute more to retirement accounts such as 401(k)s or IRAs. Take advantage of catch-up contributions if you are over the age of fifty.

Implementing these measures will help you improve your financial situation and feel more assured about your retirement readiness.

Chapter 12:

The First Year of Retirement

The first year of retirement can be an exhilarating but tough change.
The following are some crucial points to consider:

1. Financial adjustments.
- **Budgeting:** Make a precise budget to control your costs. Track your expenditures to verify you're living within your means and making adjustments as needed.
- **Income Sources:** Identify all of your income sources, including Social Security, pensions, and retirement savings. Ensure that you understand the schedule and amount of these payments.
- Maintain an emergency fund to cover unforeseen needs without using your retirement funds.

2. Lifestyle changes

- **Daily Routine:** Create a new daily routine to replace the structure that the job provides. This can include leisure activities, volunteer activities, or part-time employment.
- **Wellbeing & Wellness:** Prioritize your physical and mental wellbeing. Regular exercise, a well-balanced diet, and social activities can all help you stay healthy and active.
- **Social Connections:** Maintain contact with friends and family. Consider joining a club or group to meet new people and stay socially engaged.

3. Emotional transition.

- **Persona Shift:** Transitioning to a new persona without your professional function might be difficult. Discover fresh methods of defining yourself and your mission.
- **Set goals:** Set small and long-term goals to give your days focus and meaning. This could include traveling, gaining new skills, or pursuing passions.

- **Seek Help:** If you're having trouble making the shift, don't be afraid to contact a counselor or a support group.

4. Continuous learning.
- **Stay Informed:** Stay up to date on financial news and trends so that you may make informed investing and spending decisions.
- Consider starting a new hobby or learning new skills. This can keep your mind active and give you a sense of accomplishment.

5. Review and adjust.
- **Regular Check-Ins:** To stay on track, examine your financial condition and lifestyle on a regular basis. Adjust your plans as appropriate based on your experiences and any changes in your situation.

The first year of retirement is a period of substantial transition, but with proper planning and a positive attitude, it can be a rewarding and joyful phase of life.

Adjusting to Your New Lifestyle: Financial and Emotional Changes

Navigating the first year of retirement requires considerable emotional and financial adjustments. Here are some techniques to effectively manage these shifts:

Emotional Adjustments
- **Acknowledge your feelings:** It's normal to feel a variety of emotions, including exhilaration and nervousness. Let yourself experience these feelings without judgment.
- Talk to your friends, family, or a counselor about your emotions. Sharing your experiences can provide both support and perspective.

- Establishing a daily regimen can bring structure and purpose. Include activities that you enjoy and new ones you want to try.
- Volunteering or working part-time might also help you feel productive and involved in your community.

- Set short-term and long-term goals to guide your daily activities. This could include developing new skills, traveling, or working on personal projects.
- Celebrate little accomplishments to boost your confidence and contentment with your new lifestyle.
- Stay connected by spending time with friends and family. Join clubs or groups to meet new individuals and maintain social activity.
- Consider joining a retiree support group to share your experiences and advice.

Financial adjustments
- **Budgeting:** Develop a precise budget to manage spending. Track your expenditures to verify you're living within your means and making adjustments as needed.
- Prioritize critical expenses and seek strategies to limit discretionary spending.

Review Income Sources
- Identify all of your income sources, including Social Security, pensions, and retirement savings. Understand the time and amount of these payments.

- Consider delaying Social Security benefits to enhance your monthly payments if it is financially viable.

- Maintain an emergency fund to cover unforeseen needs without using your retirement funds.
- Aim to save a minimum of six months' worth of living costs.

- Rebalance your investment portfolio to match your risk tolerance and retirement goals. Consider adopting a more cautious asset allocation.
- Diversify your investments to reduce risk and mitigate market volatility.

Managing feelings of loss or uncertainty

- **Redefine Your Identity:** Retirement typically leads to a transformation in identity. Discover fresh methods to distinguish yourself beyond your work function.
- Engage in activities that make you happy and fulfilled, whether it's a hobby, volunteering, or learning something new.

- Maintaining physical and mental wellness is key to staying active. Regular exercise, a well-balanced diet, and social activities can all help you stay healthy and active.
- Mindfulness or meditation can help you manage stress and increase emotional well-being.

By addressing both the emotional and financial sides of retirement, you can live a satisfying and balanced life.

Tracking Your Spending: Ensuring You Stay on Budget

Steps to Track Spending

- List your monthly expenses, such as housing, utilities, groceries, transportation, healthcare, and entertainment.
- To better understand where your money goes, categorize expenses as essential or discretionary.

- Create a zero-based budget that accounts for every dollar. This ensures that your revenue matches your expenses.

- To avoid financial stress, save aside funds for unforeseen needs.

- **Use Technology:** Track your spending with budgeting apps or spreadsheets. Apps such as Mint, YNAB (You Need A Budget), and Personal Capital can help automate this process.
- To stay on track with your budget, keep your spending records updated on a regular basis.

- To identify places for savings, review and adjust your spending on a monthly basis.
- Adjust your budget to reflect changes in your financial situation or aspirations.

- Consider inflation and future healthcare expenditures when establishing your budget.

Regularly rebalance your financial portfolio to ensure it is in line with your retirement goals.

Managing Unforeseen Expenses

Handling unexpected costs in the first year of retirement.

Identify Potential Unexpected Costs.
- **Hidden Housing Costs:** Create a budget for home repairs and maintenance, such as a new roof or HVAC system.
- **Healthcare Expenses:** Even with Medicare, out-of-pocket expenses for dental, vision, and hearing care can accumulate.
- **Long-term Care:** Prepare for anticipated long-term care needs, which can be costly.
- **Family Emergencies:** Be prepared to help family members in crisis, such as adult children who want financial assistance.

Create a contingency plan.
- **Set aside a buffer:** Set aside a portion of your retirement savings specifically for unforeseen needs.
- **Flexible Budgeting:** You can adjust your budget to account for unexpected

costs without jeopardizing your financial plan.

Insurance Coverage.

- **Supplemental Insurance:** Consider purchasing supplemental insurance plans to supplement Medicare, such as Medigap or long-term care insurance.
- **house Warranty:** A house warranty can help with the expense of major home repairs.

Tips on Creating an Emergency Fund for Retirees

- **Determine the Correct Amount:** Aim to save six to nine months of living expenses.
- When deciding on a target amount, consider your health situation, homeownership, and family commitments.
- **Select the Right Account:** For convenience and higher interest rates, open a high-yield savings or money market account.
- Avoid tying up emergency funds in investments that may lose value or be difficult to sell soon.

- **Automate savings:** Create automated transfers from your checking account to your emergency fund to maintain constant savings.
- **Replenish as needed:** Maintain the balance of your emergency fund by reviewing it on a regular basis and replenishing it after any withdrawals.
- **Cut unnecessary expenses:** Identify and decrease discretionary expenditure to increase your emergency fund.

You may negotiate the financial challenges of retirement with greater confidence and peace of mind if you plan for unexpected costs and maintain an adequate emergency fund.

Chapter 13:

Ongoing Financial Management in Retirement

Managing funds in retirement is critical for maintaining a pleasant and sustainable lifestyle. Here are some important strategies for continuing financial management:

Budget and Expense Tracking:
- **Create a retirement budget:** Outline all projected revenue and expenses. Make regular updates to this budget to reflect changes in your financial status.
- Track your expenses to verify they are in line with your budget. This aids in determining areas where you can reduce expenditures if necessary.

- **Income Management:** Diversify income streams. Rely on a variety of income sources, including pensions,

Social Security, retirement assets, and part-time work.

- **Withdrawal Strategy:** To avoid depleting your retirement assets, maintain a prudent withdrawal rate. The 4% rule is commonly used; however, some experts recommend a more conservative percentage.

- Investment management involves balancing growth and risk in your investment portfolio through asset allocation. A popular approach is to subtract your age from 110 to determine how much of your portfolio should be invested in stocks.

- **Rebalancing:** Review and change your portfolio on a regular basis to retain the asset allocation you choose.

- Maintaining liquidity is crucial for managing cash flow. Make sure you have adequate liquid assets to meet regular expenses and unforeseen bills. This includes maintaining some of your savings in easily accessible accounts.

- Maintain an emergency fund to cover unexpected needs without jeopardizing your investment strategy.

Tax Planning:

- **Efficient Withdrawals:** Plan withdrawals from both taxable and tax-advantaged accounts to reduce tax liability. Consider Roth conversions if they are helpful.
- **Required Minimum Distributions (RMDs):** To avoid penalties, be aware of the RMD laws for retirement accounts.

- Plan for healthcare expenses such as premiums, out-of-pocket charges, and long-term care.
- **Insurance:** Examine and renew insurance plans to ensure adequate coverage for health, life, and property.

- Maintain up-to-date estate planning papers, including wills and trusts. This covers wills, trusts, and beneficiary designations.

- **Power of Attorney:** If you are unable to manage your finances, delegate responsibility to a trusted individual.

Following these principles allows retirees to efficiently manage their finances, resulting in a stable and comfortable retirement. Regularly evaluating and revising your financial plan is critical for adapting to new circumstances and staying financially healthy.

Revisiting Your Plan Every 1-2 Years

Regularly reviewing and revising retirement plans is critical for various reasons:

- **Adapt to Life Increases:** Health concerns, increases in living expenditures, and unexpected financial windfalls can all have a substantial impact on your retirement strategy. Regular assessments guarantee that your plan remains relevant to your present position.
- **Market fluctuations:** Financial markets are volatile. Periodic changes help to limit risks and capitalize on growth possibilities, ensuring that your investments are balanced and in line with your risk tolerance.
- **Legislative Changes:** Tax laws and retirement account restrictions may

change. Staying current guarantees compliance and maximizes tax efficiency.

- **Inflation:** The expense of living rises over time. Regular adjustments help to maintain your purchasing power and ensure that your savings last until retirement.
- **Healthcare Needs:** As you age, your healthcare requirements and prices may grow. Regularly updating your strategy ensures that you are ready for these charges.

Schedule for Financial Checkups

- **Annual Review:** Monitor your budget and expenses to ensure they correspond with retirement goals.
- **Investment Portfolio:** Review your asset allocation and rebalance if necessary.
- **Tax Planning:** Evaluate your current tax condition and plan for the following year.

- **Semi-Annual Review of Income Sources:** Examine the performance of your income streams, including pensions, Social Security, and investments.

- **Healthcare and Insurance:** Check your healthcare coverage and insurance policies to ensure they fit your requirements.

- **Quarterly Review:** Cash Flow. Keep track of your financial flow to ensure you have enough money to cover ongoing expenses.
- **Market Conditions:** Stay current with market movements and adapt your investment strategy as appropriate.

As needed:
- **Life Events:** Change your strategy in reaction to major life events like marriage, divorce, or the birth of a grandchild.
- **Legislative Changes:** Update your plan to reflect any changes to tax legislation or retirement account requirements.

By adhering to this timeframe, you can ensure that your retirement plan remains strong and flexible to changing circumstances, offering financial security and peace of mind during your retirement years.

How to Handle Changes in the Economy or Market

Adjusting retirement plans in reaction to economic swings is critical for financial stability. Here are some important strategies and examples to help retirees safeguard their assets and remain robust during market downturns or periods of inflation:

1. Diversify your investments.
Diversification is critical for spreading risk across multiple asset classes. This may include:

- Stocks have historically outperformed inflation in the long run. Bonds offer stability and income during market downturns.
- Real estate investments can help to protect against inflation.

Commodities: Investing in commodities such as gold might provide protection against inflation.

2. Rebalance Your Portfolio Regularly

Market movements may cause your asset allocation to shift. Regular rebalancing ensures that your portfolio remains in line with your risk tolerance and investing objectives.

3. Consider inflation-protected investments.

Treasury Inflation-Protected Securities (TIPS) are one type of investment that can help you protect your purchasing power during times of inflation.

4. Maintain a cash reserve.

Having an emergency fund might provide liquidity during market downturns, preventing you from selling investments at a loss.

5. Optimize Withdrawal Strategies.

- **Follow the 4% rule:** Aim to withdraw no more than 4% of your retirement savings each year, allowing for inflation.
- **Strategic withdrawals:** During downturns, consider withdrawing from more solid investments to prevent losing money while selling stocks.

6. Reduce expenses.

Cutting needless expenses will help you maximize your retirement savings. This could include downsizing your home, limiting discretionary spending, or finding ways to save money on healthcare.

7. Stay informed and adaptable.

Stay current with economic changes and be prepared to adjust your strategy as needed. Working with a financial advisor can provide individualized assistance and assist you in navigating challenging market situations.

Examples of Resilience in Different Market Conditions

- **During Inflation:** Increase your exposure to stocks and real estate, which often do well in inflationary circumstances.
- During a recession, focus on bonds and other fixed-income investments for stability and income.
- **Market Volatility:** Keep your portfolio diversified and avoid making rash decisions based on short-term market fluctuations.

Implementing these methods allows retirees to better preserve their assets and remain robust in the face of economic changes.

Keeping Your Financial Health in Check

Maintaining financial health throughout retirement is critical to leading a comfortable and stress-free existence. Here are some advice and tactics for properly managing debt, costs, and investments:

Tips to Maintain Financial Health
1. Create a budget and track income and expenses. Understand your cash flow by listing all of your revenue and spending.

- **Prioritize needs above wants:** Prioritize critical expenses such as housing, healthcare, and groceries over luxury spending.

2. Manage Debt.
Prioritize paying off credit cards and other high-interest loans.

- **Consider refinancing:** Look into refinancing possibilities to get cheaper interest rates on your existing loans.
- **Avoid additional Debt:** Be wary of taking on additional debt, especially if it will affect your retirement savings.

3. Monitor and Adjust Investments.

- Review your portfolio on a regular basis. Ensure that your investments are consistent with your risk tolerance and retirement goals.
- Diversify your investments across asset groups to lessen risk.
- **Stay informed:** Keep up with market developments and economic situations in order to make sound decisions.

4. Control Expenses
- **Cut unnecessary costs:** Identify places where you can save costs without sacrificing quality of life.
- **Shop wisely:** Look for discounts, use coupons, and compare prices to save money.
- **Healthcare Savings:** Consider generic drugs and evaluate your health insurance options once a year.

Checklist for Financial Health Metrics
Subtracting your obligations from your assets yields your net worth.
- **Debt-to-Income Ratio:** Keep this ratio low to make debt manageable in relation to your income.

- Maintain an emergency fund with enough cash to cover 6-12 months' worth of living expenses.
- **Investment Performance:** Review your investments' performance on a regular basis and make modifications as appropriate.
- **Expense Tracking:** Monitor your monthly costs to ensure they are inside your budget.
- **Withdrawal Rate:** To prevent emptying your retirement savings too soon, withdraw no more than 4% each year.
- **Healthcare spending:** Keep track of and budget for medical expenses such as insurance premiums, out-of-pocket spending, and long-term care.
- **Income Sources:** Make sure you have numerous income sources, such as pensions, Social Security, and investment income.

By following these suggestions and constantly reviewing these financial health metrics, you may ensure a stable and safe financial status during your retirement.

Chapter 14:

Glossary of Key Retirement Terms

The following is a useful dictionary for all those retirement planning phrases that can often feel like a maze:

★ **Annuities:** These are financial products that provide a consistent income stream, usually for retirees. You make an investment and are paid on a regular basis.

★ **Asset Allocation:** This is the method of separating your investing portfolio into multiple asset categories, such as stocks, bonds, and cash, in order to balance risk and reward based on your objectives and risk tolerance.

★ **Required Minimum Distributions (RMDs):** Are the annual withdrawal amounts from retirement accounts (e.g., IRAs and 401(k)s) beginning at age 72 (or 70½ if reached before January 1, 2020). Failure to take an RMD can result in significant fines.

★ **Diversification:** Diversification is a risk management approach that incorporates a wide range of investments into a portfolio. The premise is that a diversified portfolio will, on average, generate higher returns while posing less risk than any individual investment within the portfolio.

★ **Beneficiary:** The person or entity you name to receive benefits from a retirement account, life insurance policy, or estate when you die.

★ **Portfolio:** A portfolio is a collection of investments owned by an individual or entity.

★ **Risk tolerance:** Risk tolerance is the level of variability in investment returns that an investor is willing to accept. This varies with age, income, financial goals, and personal risk tolerance.

★ **Estate planning:** Estate planning is preparing duties to manage an individual's asset base in the event of incapacitation or death. It covers the transfer of assets to heirs and the payment of estate taxes.

★ **Inflation:** The rate at which the overall level of prices for goods and services rises, reducing buying power. It is critical to factor in inflation while planning for retirement to guarantee that your investments retain their value over time.

★ **Individual Retirement Account (IRA):** A tax-advantaged savings account that allows individuals to save and invest for retirement.

★ **Roth IRA:** An IRA in which you contribute after-tax cash so your assets grow tax-free and you can withdraw tax-free in retirement.

★ **401(k):** An employer-sponsored retirement savings plan in which employees can save and invest a portion of their paycheck before taxes are deducted.

★ **Pension:** A pension is a retirement plan in which an employer contributes to a pool of assets set aside for a worker's future benefits. The pool of assets is invested on the employee's behalf, and the earnings provide income to the worker at retirement.

★ **Social Security:** Benefits for retirement, disability, and survivorship are provided by the federal program known as Social Security. Benefits are dependent on the individual's earnings history.

★ **Inflation-Protected Securities:** Bonds that provide protection against inflation. Their principle and interest payments climb in line with inflation, preserving the investor's purchasing power.

Conclusion

I appreciate you completing this journey with me. I sincerely appreciate you sticking with it until the finish and, more importantly, using the principles and techniques we discussed. Your dedication to ensuring a brighter, more stable future is admirable.

If you found this guide helpful, please consider providing an honest review. Your opinion not only benefits other readers but also helps to improve future editions.

Key takeaways:

- Annual evaluations help to keep your retirement plan up to date.

- **Diversification:** Ensure that your investments are distributed across multiple asset classes.

- Adjust your goals when your circumstances change.

- **Stay Informed:** Continue to educate yourself on retirement planning.

- **Professional Advice:** Do not be afraid to seek professional help when needed.

Checklist:

☐ Make an annual evaluation of your retirement strategy.

☐ Rebalance your portfolio as needed.

☐ Regularly review your goals and financial strategy.

☐ Keep track of your funds and modify donations as needed.

☐ Review and make changes to your estate planning documents.

Your future self will appreciate the time and effort you put into preparation today. Remember that a well-thought-out retirement plan is the foundation for a rewarding and worry-free retirement. Keep moving forward and stay on track!

Thank you again for reading this book. Your path to a safe retirement is only beginning, and

I am delighted to have been a part of it. Here's to a future full of peace, purpose, and wealth!